# Turning Learning Inside Out

# Turning Learning Inside Out

*A Guide for Using Any Subject*
*to Enrich Life and Creativity*

Herbert L. Leff and Ann Nevin

Zephyr
Press

Tucson, Arizona

Turning Learning Inside Out
A Guide for Using Any Subject to Enrich Life and Creativity

Grades: All ages

© 1994 by Zephyr Press
Printed in the United States of America

ISBN 1-56976-000-4

Editors: Stacey Lynn and Stacey Shropshire
Cover design: David Fischer
Design and production: Nancy Taylor
Typesetting: Casa Cold Type, Inc.
Back cover photographs: William Dilillo and Dennis Margeson

Zephyr Press
P.O. Box 66006
Tucson, Arizona 85728-6006

Library of Congress Cataloging-in-Publication Data

Leff, Herbert L., 1944-
   Turning learning inside out : a guide to using any subject to
enrich life and creativity / Herb Leff and Ann Nevin.
      p.  cm.
   Includes bibliographical references.
   ISBN 1-56976-000-4
   1. Creative thinking—Problems, exercises, etc.   2. Active
learning—Problems, exercises, etc.   3. Teaching—Problems,
exercises, etc.   4. Self-actualization (Psychology)—Problems,
exercises, etc.   I. Nevin, Ann.   II. Title.
LB1062.L44    19443                         94-11062

*What is common to all humans in history is problems, problems, and more problems. If you are good at problem solving, you do not eventually arrive at Utopia; you get ever more difficult, more comprehensive, more incisively stated problems to solve.*

—R. Buckminster Fuller

# Contents

# Preface

Why did we write this book? Essentially, we wrote this book to invite and entice teachers to join us in exploring ways to bring learning to life. Our aim was not only to make learning a *lively* experience, but also to help all learners bring academic knowledge into everyday life in ways that could significantly enrich their real-life experience and thinking.

With this broad goal in mind, we drew liberally on Herb's twenty-something years of research and teaching in metacognition, creativity enhancement, and utopian psychology (studying mental, behavioral, and social processes for optimizing the quality of life). We also enfolded Ann's comparable experience in the areas of collaborative education and effective pedagogy (what works for teachers and students). Along the way, Herb, with consultation from Ann and others (see Leff et al. 1993), spent several years developing an "inside-out" program in a college-level introductory psychology course. In addition, we worked both individually and as a team with many K–12 teachers to explore how our newfangled ideas would play out in practice across grades and subject areas.

The upshot is the book you now hold. Most of all, we want this book to be of genuine and significant use to you—and through you to your students (and through them, to still other people as well). We've designed this book for your own personal empowerment as well as for your students' empowerment. The special cognitive techniques we discuss and the specific questions and suggestions we pose can help you enrich your own experience and problem solving as well as help you devise teaching innovations for your students' benefit. Happily, it also turns out that the more you employ any approach in your own life, the better you will be able to convey it to others.

We envision learning and teaching as enlivening adventures for all involved, mind-expanding treasure hunts that continuously yield real-life applications and enrichments. The power of our approach ultimately derives from helping students to adopt evocative and diverse perspectives, drawing on what they learn in school to focus outward with newfound vision and creativity. "Turning learning inside out" means treating *any* curriculum as an endless fountain of new ideas with potential for refreshing the lives of everyone they touch. We are delighted you are joining us on this quest.

# Acknowledgments

Any book is ultimately a team effort, and we would like to mention and thank some of the folks who have helped and worked with us as we developed this project. First, we thank the teachers, far too numerous to name here individually, who have taken our courses and workshops on "inside-out education" over the past few years. We can only hope that these incredibly imaginative and dedicated individuals have learned as much from us as we have from them. (You'll run into a few of them in the pages of this book, but the many who are not explicitly mentioned also inspired us as we wrote and revised.) We also express our deep appreciation for the creative and highly informative work of our university students as we developed and fine-tuned the inside-out approach in numerous psychology and education courses. We especially appreciate our students' cooperation and input as we learned along with them how best to put our ideas into practice.

In addition, we would like to thank our spouses, Ellen and Rolf, for their patience and their advice as we brought this book into being. Their moral support, as it has been on so many projects in the past, was truly invaluable.

For this particular project, we would also like to extend thanks to John Clarke, Marcia Croll, Jeanine Cogan, and Don Meeker for their generous and extremely helpful advice on the manuscript at crucial times in its evolution. Our colleague Toby Fulwiler also deserves acknowledgment for his ingenuity in setting up retreats for faculty to get new writing projects started. One of the sessions was especially helpful for us.

Finally, we would like to share with you our deep admiration and appreciation for the people at Zephyr Press. They genuinely care about their authors, their readers, and the advancement of creativity and kindness in the world of education (which we believe translates into the world at large!). We would like to single out Stacey Lynn for particular praise as undoubtedly one of the most considerate editors in the publishing profession. And Joey Tanner certainly deserves a special salute for starting and leading this exemplary synergistic company.

Herb Leff
Burlington, Vermont

Ann Nevin
Phoenix, Arizona

# Overview

## Inside-Out Education

### What if . . .

- schools showed students how to turn the inside academic content of their education into an immediate and powerful resource for enriching their outside lives — for helping them solve problems creatively, enjoy using their minds, replace boredom with interest, develop empathy and open-mindedness, turn even troubles into opportunities, and live more cooperatively?

### Moreover, what if . . .

- students more often took on the role of teacher, collaborated to explore creative ways to apply what they learn, and expressed their ideas and new knowledge through art, drama, music, and creative writing?

- teachers more often took on the role of learner, team taught, visited each other's classes, generally shared and built ideas together, and had more say in educational planning, design, and management?

- students routinely applied their learning and ideas not only for their own benefit but also to assist friends, family members, and others?

Collectively, these "what ifs" form the core of our vision for turning learning inside out—for enabling students to use the inside academic content of the curriculum to enrich their lives outside school (as well as within), and for empowering both students and teachers by broadening their roles and interlacing these roles in new ways.

Our primary innovation is a strategy for using academic content to enrich creative thinking in everyday life. This strategy involves the active use of "meta-thinking"—thinking about thinking and choosing how to use one's mind. It also includes a set of specific thinking tools for enriching both the learning experience and the enjoyment and creativity of everyday life. This approach enables education to transcend its traditional focus on knowledge acquisition as an end in itself in favor of an emphasis on *using* knowledge as it is acquired. (See figures O-1 and O-2.) Moreover, students can use new learning in any field to help boost their creativity in dealing with issues that lie outside that subject area.

In support of these innovations in meta-thinking and in applying academic content in everyday life, we also propose turning many of the social processes of teaching and learning inside out. For example, students can function productively as teachers for each other in many ways—cooperative learning groups, peer tutoring and partner learning, collaboration with teachers in designing lessons. Teachers, in turn, can learn from each other, from their students' creative ideas, and from their own educational and life experiments. No doubt educational administrators could also benefit from similar broadening of roles. Finally, involving school and community members more pointedly with each other can help infuse schools with real life as well as spread new ideas into the outside world.

There are a number of significant benefits this approach can bring to education:

- Students find academic content to be more interesting and relevant to their lives when they use it to enrich their creativity and experience outside (as well as within) the classroom. Teaching and learning both become more intrinsically motivating, more fun.

- Students also gain metacognitive skills that can extend beyond using academic content. In addition to figuring out and actively using the underlying thought patterns embedded in academic disciplines, students learn and generate new life-enriching ways to think, as well as develop facility with various guidelines for creative thinking. Such skills contribute to increased self-direction, self-esteem, effective problem solving, and overall coping abilities.

- The overall strategy invites a multifaceted, active, and cooperative approach to learning. This includes a wide range of collaborative classroom activities, a mix of artistic and other modes of expression, and a far-reaching expansion of the roles of teacher and

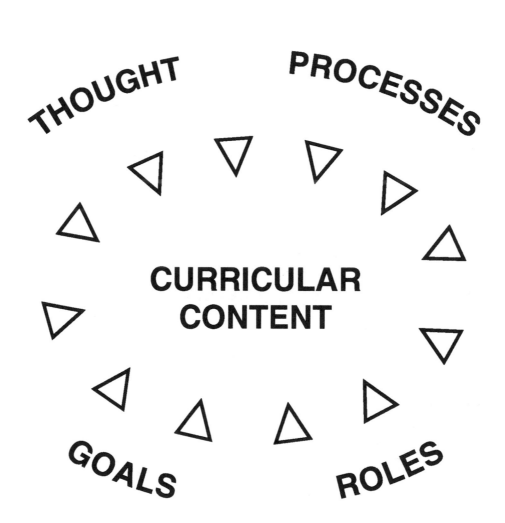

**THOUGHT** **PROCESSES**

**CURRICULAR CONTENT**

**GOALS** **ROLES**

Figure O-1

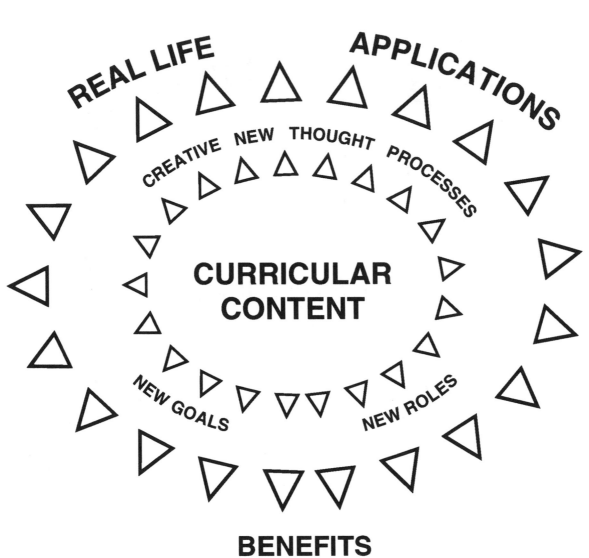

REAL LIFE APPLICATIONS

CREATIVE NEW THOUGHT PROCESSES

CURRICULAR CONTENT

NEW GOALS NEW ROLES

BENEFITS

Figure O-2

student. These changes not only make both teaching and learning interesting and effective, but also help students develop skills in cooperation and gain an expanded sense of personal responsibility and self-worth.

- The outreach activities advocated in our approach help students solidify and expand their newly developing knowledge and skills as they share these with other people. Such activities also enhance the way parents and the community view school.

It is no easy task to shift away from a model as deeply entrenched as the traditional one in education. As Thomas Kuhn (1970) has pointed out for paradigms that guide science, shifting from one underlying model to another can be a wrenching process. We have found that the shift we propose is typically much easier to understand after you have actually tried some of the thought processes involved. Fortunately, these thought processes are accessible, interesting, and useful to both teachers and students.

This book provides many examples and start-up exercises. Chapters 2 through 7 focus on various life-enriching purposes that academic content can serve. Based on the psychology of optimizing the quality of life experience (see Leff 1978), these purposes include creative problem solving, playful imaginativeness, interest and appreciation, open-mindedness, "basic enlightenment," and synergistic, cooperative thinking. We invite you to look over some of these chapters right now. Familiarity with their content will enliven your understanding of the following introductory chapter. At the end of each chapter is a mind map that summarizes that chapter.

Chapter 8 offers suggestions for teaching and learning practices that support the creativity-oriented, life-enriching uses of subject matter discussed in the earlier chapters. However, these ideas for expanding (and at times reversing) the roles of teacher and student can be helpful even within the traditional content-focused educational model.

Finally, the Epilogue takes a look at some broad personal, educational, and societal changes that could follow from widespread adoption of the inside-out approach to education. The implications of adoption are drawn mainly from projections by teachers who have experimented with inside-out practices for themselves and their students. We think the vision that emerges is very exciting and enticing—both for the big picture of education and society at large and for the more immediate level of individual schools and classrooms.

So here we go. The one essential piece of advice we have for you as you read this book is **to take a few moments to answer the questions posed in the text**. Doing so will enable you to get a taste of the types of activities our seminar and workshop participants have found so useful. As we pointed out earlier, you and others will grasp more easily this new way of applying academic content when you actually do it!

# 1

# Turning Learning Loose on Life

What are different ways students use what they learn? What might pave the way to more creative applications of knowledge? How can students get at the underlying patterns of thinking required in a subject—and then use those thought patterns to enrich their own thinking? What general purposes would help to turn learning outward to enhance everyday life?

## "Learn It to Use It!"

Even though traditional education tends to treat learning as an end in itself, it is an interesting and informative exercise to keep track for a few days of just how you actually use things you learned in school. You might consider asking your students to do so as well.

What might you find? Certainly, basic skills such as reading, writing, and simple calculating get a workout just about every day. Knowledge in areas such as geography or history comes into play for interpreting and evaluating both fiction and news. Facts and concepts gleaned in science classes may help out in sports or in do-it-yourself projects around the house. Of course, as a teacher you also use many things you learned in school as you do your job.

**NOTES**

Moreover, your students use what they learn to demonstrate knowledge in class, to prepare for the future (assuming the knowledge will be retained and actually used some time later), and perhaps to solve problems related to the content learned. These are all indeed worthy uses of what is learned in school.

Our question—and our quest—is **how can we go further in empowering ourselves and our students to develop more creative and more immediately life-enriching uses for scholastic learning?**

### The Applications Balloon

As figure 1-1 shows, our model points out five different levels of using the curriculum. The first level is not actually an outside application of subject matter but the inner core from which applications can flow. This level, *acquiring information and skills,* is of course shared with the traditional content-centered model in education. The diagram makes evident that we are not advising abandonment of such basic acquisition of knowledge. Indeed, our motto "Learn it to use it!" starts with *learn it.*

Building on this central core of academic learning, our model calls for several levels of actual application. These application levels also promote deeper interest in, understanding of, and retention of the academic subjects students apply.

Much of traditional education does include application at levels 2 and 3, although such applications are often viewed as important for supporting level 1 (acquiring knowledge) rather than as reasons for learning. Level 2 applications include using academic content to enrich awareness and understanding of the everyday world. For instance, learning about meteorology can help students to pick out different types of clouds and understand how thunder and lightning occur. Level 3 extends content use to actual problem solving in the domain of the subject area. Thus, knowledge of meteorology might be used to decide about an outing in the absence of an official weather forecast, or skill in arithmetic might be used to figure out which set of crayons is really cheapest per crayon.

# Levels of Using the Curriculum

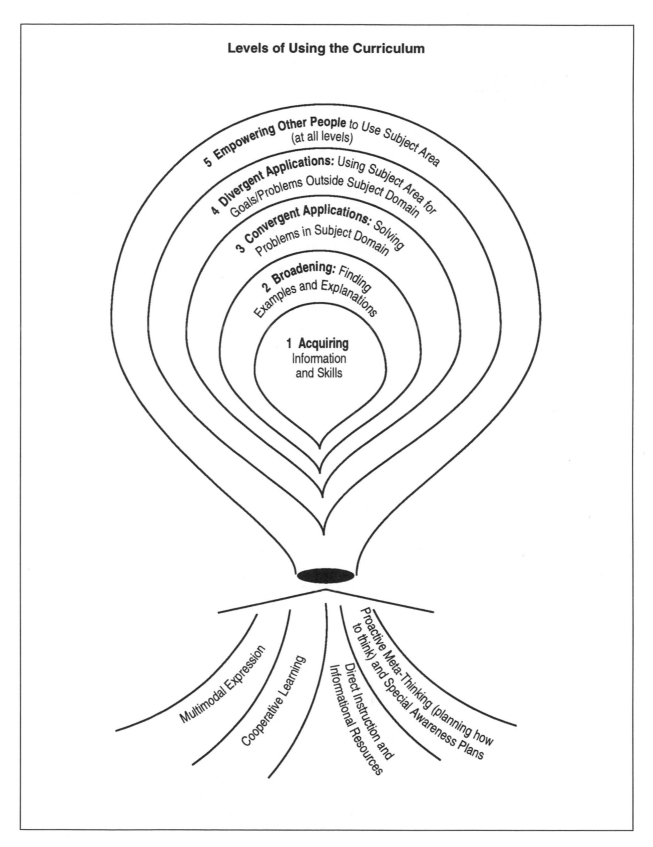

Figure 1-1

**NOTES**

Level 4, using subject matter for purposes beyond the usual bounds of a given subject area, is much less common in traditional education and represents a key emphasis in our approach. At this level, content from any discipline can be used to enrich any aspect of life or help people solve problems and think more creatively in any area the people select. At this level, meteorology, math, history, or any other subject might be used to help solve interpersonal problems, add zest to mundane tasks, or increase ability to turn troubles into opportunities.

As others who have written about transfer of learning have also observed (see, for example, Perkins 1986, 1992; Fogarty, Perkins, and Barell 1992), applying academic subject matter at this level will typically require some help. That's why we suggest bringing proactive meta-thinking and special awareness plans into play. An awareness plan is basically a specific way to use your mind—a way to think or focus attention. Proactive meta-thinking is consciously planning or choosing which awareness plans to use—deliberately deciding how to think and focus attention. (Everyday examples of such meta-thinking would be consciously deciding to count sheep to fall asleep or deliberately taking an opponent's point of view in an argument.) The special awareness plans in later chapters illustrate some powerful and varied methods for funneling academic content very usefully into all sorts of areas of life and thought.

The final level of the applications balloon is to use the skills and knowledge represented by the inner four levels to empower other people. In effect, this level of application is teaching, in the sense of facilitating other people's development of ability in applied meta-thinking, creativity, and life-enriching use of academic learning. And since teaching is very likely the best way to learn, level 5 ends up reinforcing level 1 as well. (Indeed, all the levels contribute to each other.)

The diagram also depicts various energizers feeding into the learning and application processes represented in the balloon. Central to most academic learning, of course, is instruction and informational resources (books, audio-visual aids, computer programs, and so on). Proactive meta-thinking (planning how to think), as just noted, forms the basis for wide-ranging creative use of academic content. Cooperative learning includes a variety of ways students (and teachers) can work together. These are discussed in depth in chapter 8 and also illustrated in our sample lesson plans in later chapters. "Multi-modal expression" refers to use of a wide range of sensory and communication modalities for student work and classroom activities. Examples include written or tape-recorded journals, all art modes (painting, sculpture, dance, music, drama, and so on), various forms of discussion, and just about any other way human beings can communicate constructively with each other.

We now turn to that esoteric-sounding, but very central, notion of proactive meta-thinking.

## "Think Before You Think!"

The essence of meta-processes and -states is that they are in some sense about themselves. For instance, "What is a question?" is a meta-question—a question about questions. Feeling happy about being angry at an injustice or feeling upset about being sad illustrates meta-emotions—feelings about feelings. Similarly, meta-awareness is awareness of your awareness processes (common in meditation practice, for instance). A meta-song would be a song about itself or at least about songs. Meta-education is education about education (notice this is needed for teacher certification!).

The meta-process that most concerns us for turning learning inside out is *meta-thinking*. By this we mean, as you no doubt now realize, thinking about thinking. It is roughly equivalent to the notion of *metacognition*. As theorists and researchers in this area point out (see suggested readings at the end of this chapter), metacognition can take two forms: *monitoring* your own mental processes (noticing your thoughts, knowledge, emotions, and so on) and

**NOTES**

*directing* your mental processes. The latter, executive or control, type of meta-thinking is the crucial one to inside-out education.

### Secrets of the Meta-Mode

The first secret of the meta-mode is that you empower yourself by simply realizing that you can consciously choose how to use your mind. This realization frees you to direct, if you wish, how you experience whatever life sends your way. It highlights the choice we all have to choose *what* to focus our attention on and *how* to interpret or process that input. Realizing you can choose how to experience your world empowers you to become a self-programmer. Figure 1-2 depicts a key consequence of this type of empowerment: greater ability to reach goals and to react the way you want.

To make this process especially productive, though, something more is needed. The second secret of the meta-mode is that the more effective ways to use your mind you have at your beck and call, the more true freedom of thought and reaction you have. Knowing you can choose empowers you to look for

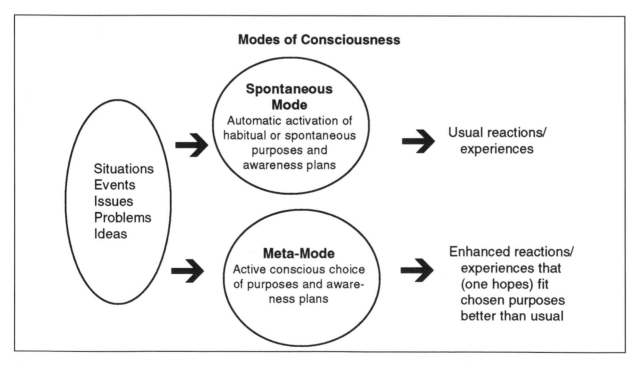

**Modes of Consciousness**

Situations
Events
Issues
Problems
Ideas

→ **Spontaneous Mode**
Automatic activation of habitual or spontaneous purposes and awareness plans

→ Usual reactions/ experiences

→ **Meta-Mode**
Active conscious choice of purposes and awareness plans

→ Enhanced reactions/ experiences that (one hopes) fit chosen purposes better than usual

**Figure 1-2**

options (Secret 1); having lots of useful options empowers you to make successful choices (Secret 2). *Awareness plan* is our term for a specific option for how to use your mind.

### Awareness Plans

A plan, according to the classic psychological work by Miller, Galanter, and Pribram (1960), is basically a way of doing something, a procedure. It is helpful to realize first that everything we do or think usually has some procedure or other that guides it. We are thus always using plans in this broad sense of procedures, even when we are not conscious of what they are and are not aware of having chosen them.

Procedures that guide our overt physical actions can be called "behavior plans." Simple examples include the physical procedures involved in getting dressed, following an exercise routine, typing, asking for a favor, or showing affection. Such plans or procedures thus guide our overt behavior (notice that even just sitting involves some sort of implicit behavior plan). By contrast, procedures guiding what we do mentally—how we go about thinking and imagining, how we deploy our attention, and thus how we generate the specific content of our ongoing awareness—can be called "awareness plans." Everyday examples include the mental procedures involved in deciding what to wear, focusing one's attention while exercising, thinking up a project or lesson, or interpreting the meaning of a compliment.

Just as we are virtually always using some sort of behavior plans or procedures to guide what we do physically, we are also always using some awareness plans (APs) or others that guide our thought processes. However, most of the time most of us are probably not aware of the awareness plans we are using, nor have we consciously created, planned, or chosen them. How often do most of us think about and consciously choose how we form judgments about other people, how we interpret what we read, how we focus our attention when doing chores, and how we go about thinking up solutions to most of the problems we encounter?

**NOTES**

**NOTES**

Most of the time, of course, our spontaneous or "normal" awareness plans see us through just fine. But it is possible and actually not very difficult to choose to use new awareness plans consciously—to choose deliberately or even to create new procedures for thinking and attending. As figure 1-2 indicates, doing so increases our ability to reach goals and shape mental (and overt) reactions in ways our automatic plans might not.

The following chapters present examples of very special awareness plans that serve a variety of life-enriching purposes. These purposes include increasing creativity, playfulness, appreciation and interest, open-mindedness, constructive coping (basic enlightenment), and synergistic, cooperative approaches to the world (see figure 1-3). Based on a wide range of psychological research and theory (see Leff 1978 and the various references throughout this book), these purposes are broad and empowering enough to contribute to practically any type of goal in some useful way. For instance, enhancing creative thinking is useful for just about any real-life problem, and open-mindedness is likely to help in any interpersonal situation.

To support these broad, life-enriching purposes we have collected a number of awareness plans that we, our students, and our research participants have found especially powerful. We started out to dub the very best of these awareness plans the "Magnificent Seven," but we ended up with many more than seven candidates for that honor. Doubtless some of the awareness plans presented in this book (or in Leff 1984) will appeal to you or to particular students much more than other plans. But the real point of our presentation is to offer useful examples of especially beneficial ways to use one's mind. Ultimately, we hope that you and your students will create and share your own magnificent APs. What we wish to emphasize is the value of being able to select from a wide palette.

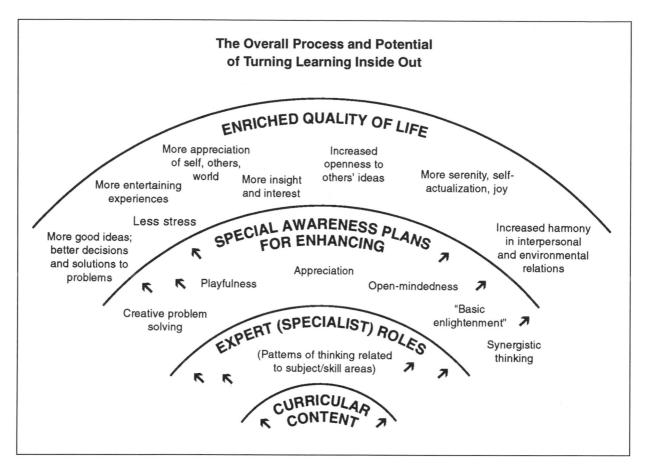

**The Overall Process and Potential
of Turning Learning Inside Out**

ENRICHED QUALITY OF LIFE

More appreciation
of self, others,
world

Increased
openness to
others' ideas

More entertaining
experiences

More insight
and interest

More serenity, self-
actualization, joy

Less stress

SPECIAL AWARENESS PLANS
FOR ENHANCING

Increased harmony
in interpersonal
and environmental
relations

More good ideas;
better decisions
and solutions to
problems

Playfulness

Appreciation

Open-mindedness

Creative problem
solving

"Basic
enlightenment"

EXPERT (SPECIALIST) ROLES

Synergistic
thinking

(Patterns of thinking related
to subject/skill areas)

CURRICULAR
CONTENT

**Figure 1-3**

## The Central Processes in
## Inside-Out Education

The main point of our inside-out approach is to use academic content to enhance life. However, the broadest types of such real-life application call for helpful cognitive bridges. The types of awareness plans discussed in later chapters provide such bridges. These APs can readily assist you and your students to relate academic content in creative ways to such goals as arousing interest (in anything you choose), solving any type of problem calling for creative thinking, and approaching any type of situation in a constructive manner.

The key technique is first to assess the underlying patterns of thinking (or specialist roles) in a subject area—and then to draw on those roles to be more creative and resourceful in using awareness plans that apply directly to life goals (see figure 1-3). One teacher suggested the delightful metaphor "chameleon thinking" to describe this process. This term strikes us as very appropriate, since each new role and AP does indeed change the complexion of one's thought and awareness.

We now take a closer look at the way this process works, but we must issue the following alert: It is much easier to do this process than it is to understand and explain it. If you haven't yet peeked, please do look ahead to some of the examples and exercises in later chapters. Our bumper sticker would read

## IT'S EASIER TO SHOW THAN TO TELL.

### An Introductory Demonstration

We now invite you to try a little demonstration exercise to get a taste of the way inside-out education turns academic knowledge into a creativity resource. Please play along with us here!

*Step 1:*  Take a look at the abstract drawing in figure 1-4 and list as many things as you can think of that the drawing could represent. (Notice that thinking up alternative meanings is an awareness plan.) Keep going until you run out of ready ideas. All set? Go! (You can use the space below for your list.)

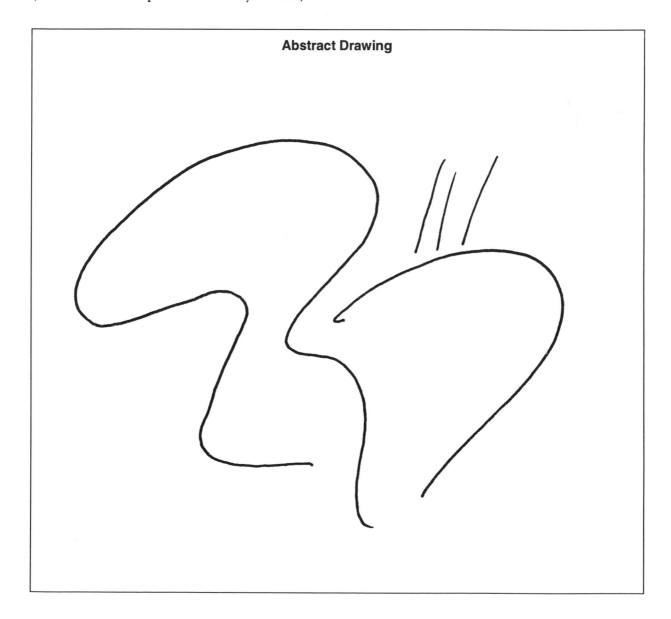

**Abstract Drawing**

*Step 2:* **(Please do not read this until you have completed Step 1!)** After you have run dry of interpretations of the drawing, try this: Ask yourself what a biologist might see in the drawing. Then ask yourself how a meteorologist might interpret the figure. How about a mathematician? A musician? Also try putting yourself in some other academic roles (perhaps a sports expert, architect, home economist, favorite novelist, or whatever you choose). For each role, what new meanings can you find for our little drawing? List them here:

**Biologist:**

**Meteorologist:**

**Mathematician:**

**Musician:**

**Sports Expert:**

**Architect:**

**Home Economist:**

**Favorite Novelist:**

_____ :

NOTES

If you are like most people, you probably found that even after you thought you had run out of possible interpretations for the drawing, merely trying on a new role readily opened the door to some new possibilities. Roles based on academic specialties turn out to be especially rich for opening up new conceptual possibilities because academic disciplines have exceptionally rich conceptual networks. Also, the more you know about any academic area, the more you can draw on those conceptual networks. (You may have noticed that subjects you know the best also yielded the most new interpretations for the drawing.)

For a variation on this demonstration, you might try picking out a common object such as a pencil sharpener or a drinking glass. Then first (without using specialist roles) think up new uses for the object. After completing your initial brainstorming, try drawing on the above (or other) specialist roles to see how many additional new uses they suggest for the same object.

There is a message here. Academic thought patterns can be a wonderful resource for new ideas about anything. How, then, can we go further in figuring out—and thus preparing to use—the patterns of thinking inherent in any particular subject area?

## Role Analysis

One powerful technique for ferreting out subject-area thought patterns is to map the mental role of a devoted specialist in the given subject. Jerome Bruner (1962) called attention to the French concept of *une deformation professionelle*, which points up the tendency of people in any profession or occupation to grow into a pattern of thinking (or set of awareness plans, if you will) shaped by the concerns of that occupation. Realtors thus may tend to look at the world in terms of property values, doctors in terms of bodily processes and health concerns, shoe salespeople in terms of footwear, and so on. How would you characterize the *deformation professionelle* of students? And of teachers?

(Please take a few moments to think up and even to jot down your own ideas—we've provided spaces—whenever you see our invitation. Doing so will greatly enrich what you get from this book.)

**NOTES**

Bruner's point may of course be an overstatement for many individuals who may well leave their professional concerns and associated awareness plans at work. We can still use the concept to help map specialist roles, however. All we need to do is figure out how a truly "professionally deformed" specialist might look at the world, and we then have a rich starting place for academically amplifying any AP we choose—and thus for increasing our creativity in achieving the purpose of the chosen awareness plan.

For academic disciplines, such specialist roles or thought patterns may be defined in terms of four key categories:

## ❶ INTERESTS

Interests are the domains of concern for the particular discipline. On what does the subject focus? What phenomena, topics, or processes would a specialist care about or notice? What might be the subject's underlying allure? Chemists, for example, are concerned with compounds, the composition of substances, and processes of molecular combination and new substance formation; perhaps they find beauty and enjoyable mental challenge in analyzing and synthesizing materials. Economists, on the other hand, focus on financial matters of all kinds and the processes of producing and exchanging goods and services. The allure of this field might lie in understanding, predicting, and perhaps influencing such complex social processes. Grammarians' interests encompass the world of sentence structure, punctuation, word usage and combinations, and spelling; the charm of this field might lie in the application of definite rules and the fun of treating punctuation marks and sentences as objects of interest in themselves. Each domain of interest suggests a new filter for thinking about the world.

## ❷ METHODS

Methods are the central techniques specialists in the field use to gather or process information—and thus to pursue their interests. What are favorite research techniques? How are new ideas or theories generated? What modes of communication or presentation are used? A biologist's methods (naturalistic observation, experimentation, computer simulation, and the like) will be very different from those of a historian or an author of children's stories. What are some of the methods involved in your own favorite subjects?

Methods used in a variety of subject areas are in themselves a stimulating source of new ways to think about any situation. In evaluating your teaching, for example, you might draw on science to think up experimental checks on your new (and old) teaching ideas. Or you might borrow from history to point toward an archival review of how your lesson plans or students' work has evolved over the years. From literary composition you might think up different forms you could use to give yourself feedback—say, a poem after each class, or perhaps a short story illustrating how you might have done things differently.

## ❸ IDEAS

Ideas are the concepts, facts, principles, and theories within the subject area. This of course is at the heart of what we normally consider to be academic content. Clearly, to get truly inside the thinking patterns of a subject specialist, you have to know at least a portion of what the specialist would know. The wider and deeper your knowledge of the subject area, the better prepared you will be to use that subject to enrich your thinking. Indeed, a key test for whether any academically enhanced awareness plan is working is whether its use leads you to want to know more about the academic area used to enrich the awareness plan so that you can use the enhanced AP even more effectively.

**NOTES**

**NOTES**

## ④ QUESTIONS

These questions are the type that a specialist in the subject area would ask. Ask yourself, "What new information would a specialist in this field like to know?" or "What types of questions might such a specialist ask about a situation or topic in which I am interested?" As chapter 4 discusses, thinking up questions is itself a very effective awareness plan for stimulating interest, and any academic area can supply a rich source of question themes. This same approach of drawing on specialists' questions can also enrich a variety of other awareness plans. For example, as we shall see in chapter 6, specialist questions can be a useful way to generate new ideas for opportunities in any situation and new approaches to learning from any set of circumstances.

### Some Sample Role Maps

To illustrate how to put all four components together, figure 1-5a through 1-5d presents some simple role maps for various academic areas and invites you to make a map of your own. We have found that sketching out such maps can be an effective aid for understanding new academic material as well as for preparing to use it to enhance awareness and behavior plans. This approach to content also helps provide an overall picture of a subject area as well as weave together the various specific topics. Most important, though, the mapping process helps learners clarify (and ultimately use) the underlying patterns of thinking within a subject field.

Important stress-reducing note: In constructing role maps, the essential point is simply to develop and clarify one's understanding of the specialist perspective being represented. There is no need to worry about getting each entry in the correct quadrant! The headings are intended mainly to help spark role insights.

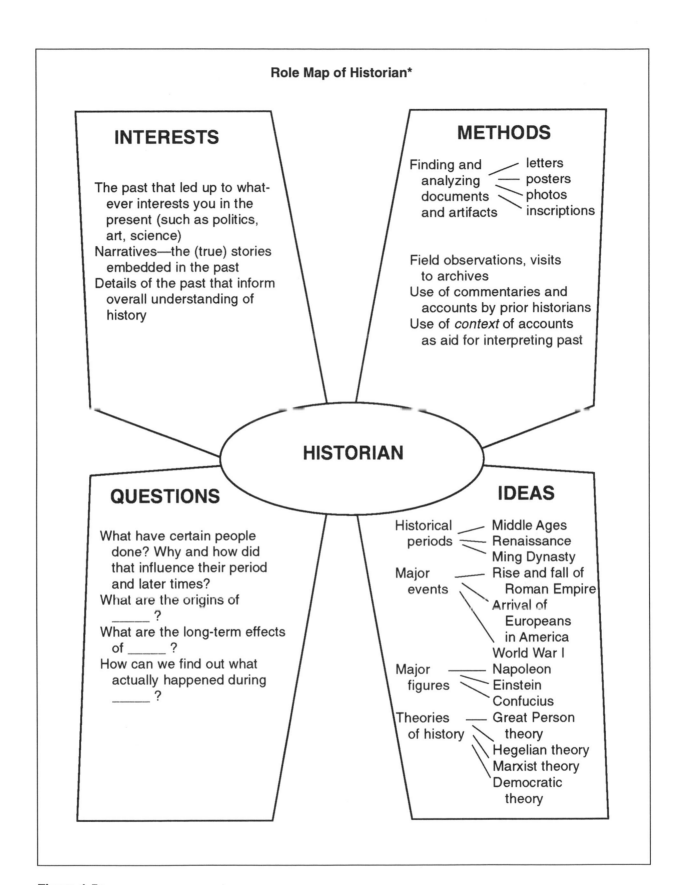

**Role Map of Historian\***

**INTERESTS**

The past that led up to whatever interests you in the
present (such as politics,
art, science)
Narratives—the (true) stories
embedded in the past
Details of the past that inform
overall understanding of
history

**METHODS**

Finding and ⎯ letters
analyzing ⎯ posters
documents ⎯ photos
and artifacts ⎯ inscriptions

Field observations, visits
to archives
Use of commentaries and
accounts by prior historians
Use of *context* of accounts
as aid for interpreting past

**HISTORIAN**

**QUESTIONS**

What have certain people
done? Why and how did
that influence their period
and later times?
What are the origins of
_____ ?
What are the long-term effects
of _____ ?
How can we find out what
actually happened during
_____ ?

**IDEAS**

Historical ⎯ Middle Ages
periods ⎯ Renaissance
        ⎯ Ming Dynasty
Major ⎯ Rise and fall of
events   Roman Empire
        Arrival of
        Europeans
        in America
        World War I
Major ⎯ Napoleon
figures ⎯ Einstein
        Confucius
Theories ⎯ Great Person
of history   theory
        Hegelian theory
        Marxist theory
        Democratic
        theory

**Figure 1-5a**

*Based in part on our interview with historian Henry Steffens.

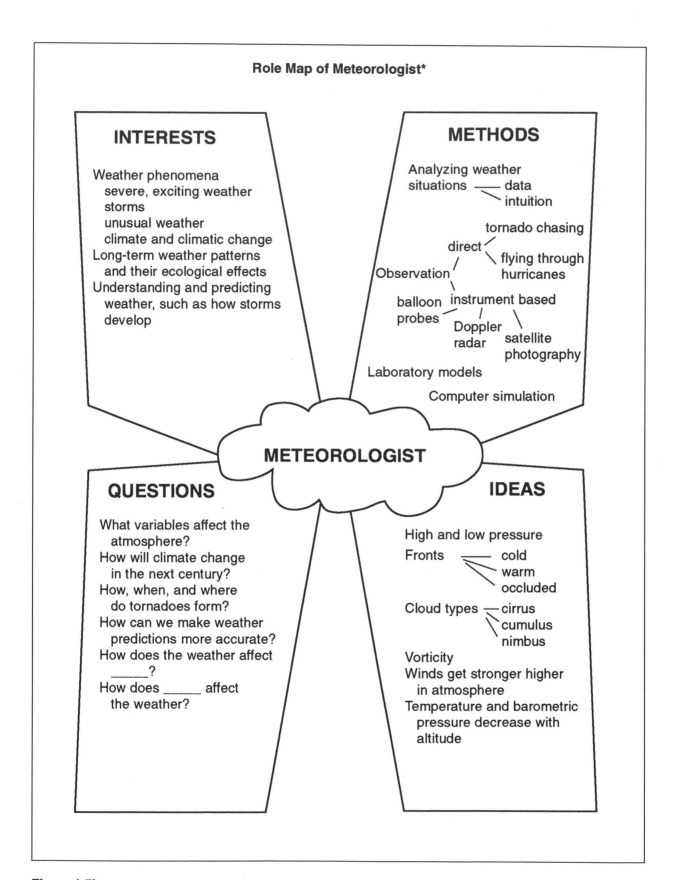

**Role Map of Meteorologist***

**INTERESTS**

Weather phenomena
    severe, exciting weather
    storms
    unusual weather
    climate and climatic change
Long-term weather patterns
    and their ecological effects
Understanding and predicting
    weather, such as how storms
    develop

**METHODS**

Analyzing weather
situations —— data
            intuition
                        tornado chasing
            direct
                        flying through
Observation              hurricanes
balloon  instrument based
probes   Doppler
         radar   satellite
                 photography
Laboratory models
        Computer simulation

**METEOROLOGIST**

**QUESTIONS**

What variables affect the
    atmosphere?
How will climate change
    in the next century?
How, when, and where
    do tornadoes form?
How can we make weather
    predictions more accurate?
How does the weather affect
    _____?
How does _____ affect
    the weather?

**IDEAS**

High and low pressure
Fronts —— cold
        warm
        occluded
Cloud types — cirrus
              cumulus
              nimbus
Vorticity
Winds get stronger higher
    in atmosphere
Temperature and barometric
    pressure decrease with
    altitude

**Figure 1-5b**

*Based in part on our interview with meteorologist Julie Gam.

# Role Map of Actor*

## INTERESTS

Being other than yourself
Experiencing the intensified
  feelings and communication
  that occur when acting
Playing
Being the focus of others'
  attention
Creating characters and
  impressions
Entertaining oneself and others
Having an impact on other people

## METHODS

Reading and analyzing scripts
Reading material *related* to
  the character or story to be
  acted out
*Doing* the types of things your
  character does—especially
  the physical things
Imagining what you would feel
  if you were your character
Rehearsing—trying out different
  ways of playing the role and
  getting feedback from other
  actors, the director, and your
  own reactions
Doing relaxation and warm-up
  exercises

## ACTOR

## QUESTIONS

What chain of events brought
  us to our present modes of
  response?
What do I need to know to bring
  this person (character) to life?
What makes this person be, feel,
  and respond this way?
How can I access, "physicalize,"
  and vocalize all of this material
  on what contributes to the
  character's response?

## IDEAS

Focus—tuning out things
  extraneous to the moment

Talking and listening as
  essence of acting

Objective—what a character
  wants (in the scene, in
  the play, in life)

Actions—play out objectives
  through your actions

Emotional recall and sense
  memory

Stage directions — upstage
  downstage
  stage left,
  right

Script scoring—"beats"
  (pieces of unified text)

**Figure 1-5c**

*Based in part on our interview with actor Margaret Schenk.

Role Map of _____ (your favorite academic area)

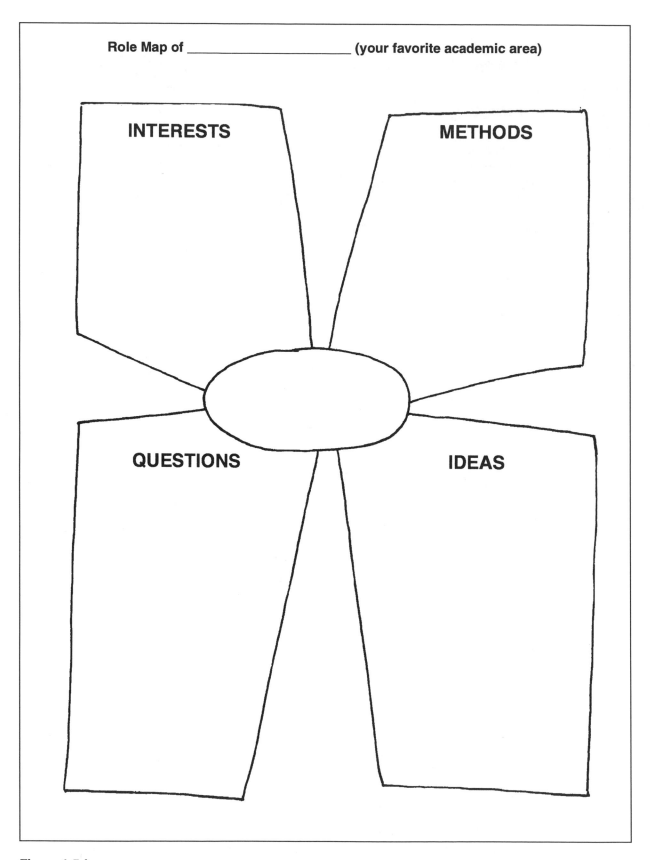

INTERESTS

METHODS

QUESTIONS

IDEAS

Figure 1-5d

## Strategies for Using Academic Roles

The next step is of course to use the thought patterns represented by specialist role maps to enhance one's own thinking and action. The specific awareness plans discussed in later chapters provide sample bridges for bringing academic thought patterns into everyday life in usefully creative ways. The key to using a specialist role in this way is simply to ask what advice the specialist would give you for enhancing or using these or other awareness plans.

Here are some general guidelines to keep in mind whenever you turn education inside out in the way we are suggesting:

- **Use more than one academically derived role.** Whenever you or your students use specialist thinking to solve problems or to get more out of using special awareness plans, pick several different roles from the subject matter that you teach. (For still more diversity, you might on occasion also draw on roles from other subject areas as well.) Using more than one specialist role will contribute to increased mental flexibility. It will also help to differentiate the subject-based thought patterns from each other and from one's own normal, spontaneous approaches. Perhaps most valuable, using multiple consultant roles readily leads to more than one right answer—a key element in creative thinking according to theorists such as Roger von Oech and Edward de Bono (see suggested readings at the end of chapter 2).

- **Make sure your students understand the concepts and roles correctly before applying the roles.** Actually, even incorrectly understood roles may still be useful for sparking creative ideas—but students will tend to learn well what they apply, so it pays to check their understanding first. In addition, the more accurately and thoroughly students understand the ideas from a subject area, the richer will be their potential uses of the material.

**NOTES**

**NOTES**

Devoting some care to making role maps or otherwise delving into the specialist roles to be used definitely pays off in more productive and meaningful applications.

- **Use academic content in inside-out fashion yourself.** Just as teaching something is a great way to learn it, actively using something yourself is a great aid for teaching its use to others. Using academic thought patterns to enrich your own thinking really does work. So not only will you spark your own creative thought, but you will also boost your value as a role model and source of hands-on wisdom for your students. In addition, to see what we are getting at in this new approach, it helps a lot to work from the inside out—to experience what using academic content in the ways we propose actually does for your thinking before presenting it to your students. For instance, in doing the short start-up exercises (usually flagged by our ✍ invitation), you might often find it useful to substitute specialist roles based specifically on your own areas of teaching or special interest for the more generic roles (such as geographer or mathematician) that we offer as samples.

- **As much as possible, give your students choices.** Probably the most important single lesson we have learned in developing inside-out programs is the importance of allowing students as much choice as possible. We realize that most teachers will not have the luxury of offering alternative versions of their classes, but it is still possible to offer students significant options within almost any class. You might offer alternative paper or journal assignments, choice of topics or techniques for projects, options for varied types of goals or subject matter to be applied, and so on. The principle to bear in mind is that choice breeds intrinsic motivation (see Deci and Ryan 1985 for a thorough discussion).

## The Role of Purpose
## (or the Purpose of Roles)

Chapters 2 through 7 offer suggestions for how
academic content can excite creative thinking for a
variety of life-enriching purposes: creativity, playful
imagination, interest and appreciation, open-
mindedness, basic enlightenment, and synergistic
thinking. Implicit in our chapter organization is the
notion that it is important to have a purpose when
applying academic content—or when consciously
trying out any new awareness plan, for that matter.
We have found that it is crucial for learners to have a
reason for any mental effort. Of course, the reason
can be as simple and open-ended as "to generate an
interesting new experience." Or the purpose can be
very specific or intricate, such as "to make doing this
math homework more fun" or "to figure out how to
resist peer pressure to try drugs without losing
friends."

The following chapters are organized around
some very broad purposes—appreciation and interest,
creativity enhancement, and the like—that we find can
apply to virtually any specific goal. Our intent, however, is not so much to point toward the goals as it is
to highlight a way that academic content—what is
learned in school—can be used to enhance thinking
for any purpose learners choose.

As you read the rest of this book, we do hope that
you will try out the various exercises and respond to
the questions along the way. Even more important,
though, we hope you will think up your own new ways
to use academic subject areas to enrich your life and
to empower your students to do the same for their
lives. The more you experiment with this inside-out
approach to teaching and learning, the more depth
and possibility you will discover.

**NOTES**

# Summary Mind Map

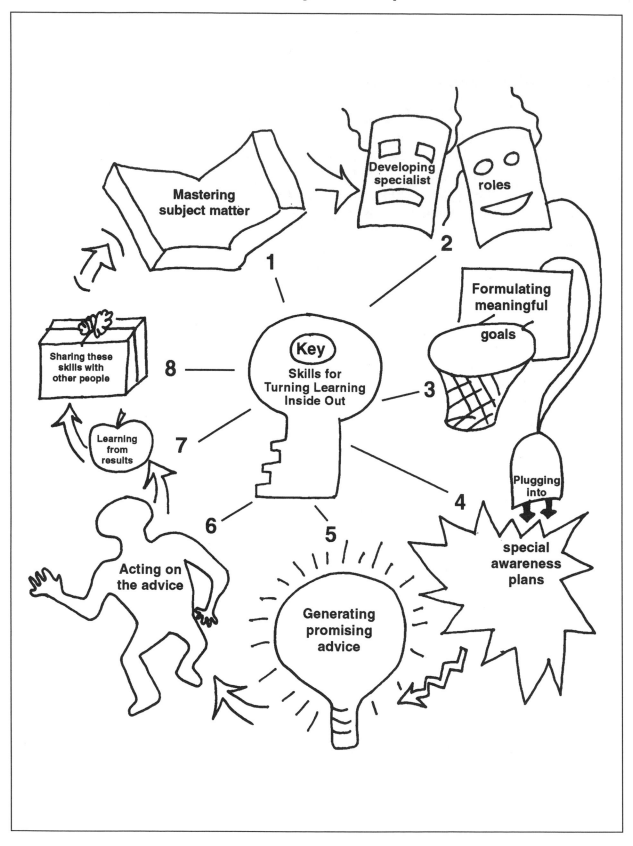

## Suggested Readings on Meta-Thinking

Barell, John. *Teaching for Thoughtfulness: Classroom Strategies to Enhance Intellectual Development.* New York: Longman, 1991.
> Detailed, richly informative guide to encouraging students to be inquiring, self-reflective critical thinkers.

Bruner, Jerome. *Acts of Meaning.* Cambridge: Harvard University Press, 1990.
> Highly insightful and awareness-provoking discussion of how fundamental the creation of meaning is in human cognition and experience.

Clarke, John. *Patterns of Thinking: Integrating Learning Skills in Content Teaching.* Boston: Allyn and Bacon, 1990.
> Wide-ranging discussion of educating for thinking skills, with special emphasis on the use of graphic organizers to assist thinking processes.

Costa, Arthur, ed. *Developing Minds.* 2 vols. Alexandria, Va.: Association for Supervision and Curriculum Development, 1991.
> Major compendium of strategies, tactics, and theoretical considerations for the teaching of thinking—a modern classic.

Hofstadter, Douglas R. *Gödel, Escher, Bach: An Eternal Golden Braid.* New York: Basic Books, 1979.
> Very challenging reading, but excellent for illustrating self-reflective (meta-mode) processes and the strange loops they can involve.

Kuhn, Thomas S. *The Structure of Scientific Revolutions.* 2nd ed. Chicago: University of Chicago Press, 1970.

Langer, Ellen J. *Mindfulness.* Reading, Mass.: Addison-Wesley, 1989.
> Popularly written account of Langer's research and theory on the value of mindfulness—attention to new categories and information, alternative perspectives, and process rather than merely end products.

Nelson, Thomas O., ed. *Metacognition: Core Readings.* Boston: Allyn and Bacon, 1992.
> An excellent, varied collection of both theoretical and empirical articles, covering a very wide range of topics in metacognition.

Perkins, David N. *Knowledge as Design.* Hillsdale, N.J.: Lawrence Erlbaum, 1986.
> Thought-provoking discussion of the purposeful, functional nature of knowledge, interlaced with very helpful advice for teachers.

Tiedt, Iris M., Jo Ellen Carlson, Bert D. Howard, and Kathleen S. Oda Watanabe. *Teaching Thinking in K–12 Classrooms: Ideas, Activities, and Resources.* Boston: Allyn and Bacon, 1989.
> Rich collection of ideas and lesson plans on the teaching of thinking throughout the curriculum, written by four teachers who clearly know what they are talking about.

Udall, Anne J., and Joan E. Daniels. *Creating the Thoughtful Classroom: Strategies to Promote Student Thinking.* Tucson, Ariz.: Zephyr Press, 1991.
> Valuable advice for practical classroom techniques and ways to evaluate higher-level thinking.

Weinert, Franz E., and Rainer H. Kluwe, eds. *Metacognition, Motivation, and Understanding.* Hillsdale, N.J.: Lawrence Erlbaum, 1987.
> Informative, wide-ranging academic discussions of various aspects of metacognition.

**2**

# Learning for Creative Problem Solving

What lies at the core of creative thinking? How can
students use school subjects to activate their creativity
in dealing with issues that matter to them? What
special awareness plans facilitate this process?

## Creativity

What might bumper stickers say to get across the inner
core of creativity? Here are a few possibilities:

IT'S GOTTA BE NEW AND GOOD

WE'RE ALL FULL OF IT!

BUT THERE'S ROOM FOR MORE

CONNECT AND MULTIPLY

I BRAKE 4 ASSUMPTIONS

MAKE IDEAS, NOT WAR

LOOK OUT—
I HAVE MULTIPLE PERSPECTIVES

EVEN IF IT'S RIGHT,
DON'T SIT TIGHT

What's going on here? What principles of creativity are we proposing? In order of the bumper stickers:

First, we define *creativity* as the production of new—and in some way useful or "good"—things or ideas. (This is typical of how most creativity researchers and theorists regard the topic these days; see suggested readings at the end of this chapter.)

Second, everybody is creative. Of course, people differ in the quantity and quality of their ideas, but every human being performs all kinds of creative thought processes in the course of everyday life. Just think of the new and useful ideas you generate as you devise or revise lesson plans and the new and useful ideas your students generate as they compose stories or play tricks on each other.

Third, creativity skills can be learned. True, there is an almost magical quality to the mental leaps involved in producing any new idea or connection. But there are ways to increase the likelihood of making productive new connections, trying new perspectives, and supporting other components of creative thinking.

Fourth, our final five bumper sticker slogans are intended to illustrate key ingredients in creative thinking:

- Forming new mental connections, especially combinations of things not normally linked

- Breaking (or perhaps just "braking" or "slowing down") assumptions—particularly helpful when the assumptions are our hidden ones (such as that numbers cannot stand 4 words?)

- Generating a multitude of possibilities (and, as the "NOT WAR" part of the slogan hints, forming new ideas by building constructively on others' ideas)

- Trying out many new perspectives; in effect, using a variety of guiding awareness plans or mental roles

**NOTES**

- Figuring out improvements in things that seem all right as well as finding solutions for "problems"; also, looking for new solutions even after you've thought of one (what Roger von Oech refers to as "the second right answer")

All this, of course, is only part of the story. For instance, Teresa Amabile (1983, 1989), a creativity researcher at Brandeis University, has cogently argued that creativity involves three main assets: (1) knowledge and skill in the area in which one wishes to be creative, (2) skill in using creativity-enhancing procedures, and (3) intrinsic motivation—especially when *not* combined with extrinsic motivation that feels constraining (see also Amabile 1993).

Amabile's main area of investigation has been the seemingly crucial role motivation plays in creativity. Factors such as promise of reward, threat of punishment, competition, and restricted choice all can interfere with creativity if the person is intrinsically motivated by the task to begin with. Clearly, if Amabile is right, much of what goes on in traditional education could play havoc with the creative process.

There is hope, however. Even in the face of "extrinsic constraints" such as competitive grading, testing, and enforced assignments, students with a genuine intrinsic interest can maintain their creative impetus. A useful approach Amabile suggests is for students to remind themselves consciously of their sources of inner interest in a subject area (such as how much fun it can be to play with words, to read about the past, or to conduct experiments). Another tack is to explore ways to use subject matter constructively even when tests and grading are ultimately involved as well. The inside-out approach to education presented in this book could thus yield a bonus of increasing creativity by exciting intrinsic motivation as well as by teaching special creativity-enhancing awareness plans.

In addition, any approach in education that boosts interest in subject matter should foster growth in knowledge and skill. One of our key tests for the success of using academic roles and content as advised in this book is that students will develop more interest in the subject areas they apply. So, taking all three of Amabile's factors into account—creative-thinking skills, intrinsic motivation, and substantive knowledge—inside-out education offers a promising path to boosting creativity.

## Content and Creativity

Our primary focus in this chapter is on using subject matter as a resource for being more creative. As we pointed out in chapter 1, academic content can be applied at many levels. To spark creativity and to expand the range of problems to which academics can apply, we especially recommend level 4 in our balloon diagram (see figure 1-1): applying subject content to goals and problems that lie outside any obvious relation to that subject area. Use math to help think up new ways to deal with loneliness; see how history could spur new approaches to finding a part-time job; draw on biology for new ways to cure "senioritis." Is there a simple way to use any subject to help solve any type of problem calling for creative thinking?

Our answer is YES! A simple, yet extremely powerful, procedure is to ask what ideas a particular type of academic specialist (mathematician, geographer, biologist, or whatever) would offer for solving your problem. Additionally, imaginative, creativity-assisting roles can be derived directly from subject content, such as particular historical or literary characters or even personifications of concepts or objects of study. Indeed, the most effective kind of awareness plan for boosting creativity may well be to take on a variety of mental roles. And academic subject areas are a splendid source of roles that are rich in conceptual depth and complexity. Of course, the more you know about a given subject area, the better you can use this approach, but even a slight familiarity with a subject can be used to evoke new ideas.

Let's try it right now. Select an issue—one that matters to you—for which you would like to generate some useful new ideas. For example, you might pick the issue of creating more enjoyable homework assignments.

**NOTES**

**Your issue:**

```

```

Now ask what different academic specialists might suggest for dealing with your issue. For instance, on the homework issue an economist might suggest creating a "homework bank" where students deposit their own ideas for assignments, earn "interest" on the basis of how interesting their ideas are to other students, and borrow or withdraw assignments approved by the CEO (you). Alternatively, a computer scientist might suggest homework assignments that build "programmatically" on each other or that involve a computer-game format of some kind—perhaps a role-playing adventure game, where the characters and scenarios are based on the academic content.

**Your ideas for your issue, based on academic roles:**

```

```

Notice that the initial ideas each academic role generates may or may not be full-fledged solutions for your issue, but they are at least likely to point your mind in new directions. As in the case of our abstract drawing demonstration in figure 1-4, each new role calls up a new conceptual framework—a new launching pad for generating potentially useful ideas. However, the ultimate payoff of effective solutions may come only after you build on the initial ideas suggested by the role. As we shall explore in depth later in this chapter, most awareness plans for boosting creative thinking involve a similar two-step process: first generate ideas based on a new way of thinking, then build on those ideas to create effective solutions. A bumper sticker for this process might read

# FIRST NEW, THEN GOOD.

Before proceeding to the more complex creativity plans, though, let's take a look at some examples of how teachers at different grade levels can help their students use simple academic role-taking to spark creative problem solving.

──────── **AN EXAMPLE FROM EARLY ELEMENTARY SCHOOL** ────────

Even young children are quite capable of using roles based on their curriculum to help solve real-life problems more creatively. For instance, Diane Happy and Karen Pearo introduced their combined first- and second-grade class to our role-taking process by getting their students to brainstorm how the title characters from *Puss 'n Boots* and *Pinocchio* would solve various problems that concerned the students. These teachers prepared their class by first asking the children to brainstorm ideas alone and then, working in small groups, to take off their own "thinking caps" and put on Puss's thinking cap (making "kitten ear" motions to get in the mood) or Pinocchio's (with "long nose" motions for emphasis). Each group recorded its ideas on a record sheet provided by the teachers and also reported orally to the rest of the class.

Here are a few sample problems and responses:

| Problem | Puss Solution | Pinocchio Solution |
| --- | --- | --- |
| I don't like peas but must eat them at dinner. | Ask for corn instead. | Spill them. |
| Dad keeps changing TV channel with remote. | Push AR button (disables channel changing) on remote. | Be funny so he'll drop the remote control. |
| Cat throws up on floor. | Take him to vet. | Tape his mouth shut. |

In discussing these Puss and Pinnochio solutions, the class created a "Redesign Your Supper" plan for dealing with despised vegetables. A number of the students went home and, following the Puss approach, politely asked for an alternative vegetable. When these kids reported that this actually worked, several more students followed suit, and some even used variations of the approach at their baby-sitters' homes. And even the teachers found the Puss solution for the TV remote to be effective.

Although the roles used here were not academic specialists per se, they were based directly on what the students were studying. Moreover, the teachers made sure their students were dealing with their own real-life issues by getting the students to generate the problems and assisted the students in "getting into" the roles (by discussing the two books beforehand and by using physical movements and the "thinking cap" metaphor). The teachers and students also seemed to think that some of the solutions generated by the use of these roles were more creative and effective than were their earlier efforts to grapple with the problems.

## AN EXAMPLE FROM THE FIFTH GRADE

Working with her fifth-grade class, Susan Underhill was able to develop a series of short inside-out lessons that gave both her and her students a new faith in the power of academic roles to solve real-life problems. Susan began the lesson series by holding a class discussion about the ideas and concepts that went with various academic roles, such as mathematician, historian, scientist, language arts expert, and physical education teacher. To her delight, the students displayed an impressive grasp of the academic content for each role. To aid in future applications, the class created large posters listing key ideas associated with each role. These posters were tacked up on the walls around the room.

Susan then asked the class to list problems of genuine concern to them. Issues such as war and peace (the Persian Gulf War with Iraq was occurring at the time), drug abuse, and teenage pregnancy cropped up.

Next, working in small groups, the students explored how a variety of people in academic roles would suggest dealing with some of the problems. On the issue of drug abuse, for instance, Susan's students drew on the role of mathematician to raise various quantitative questions ("How many drugs do kids do a year?" "Do you do drugs the same time every day?") and generated solutions such as "You can give them money to do something else" and "You can give them fake drugs." Building on the role of scientist, the students generated observations and suggestions such as "Kids do drugs to experiment," "Some drugs come from plants," "Take out all the plants that are made into drugs," and "Kids can do an activity or do sports instead of drugs." Building on that last idea of alternatives to drugs, the students also listed ideas for ways to have fun without using drugs that each academic role might suggest.

## ———————— AN EXAMPLE FROM JUNIOR HIGH SCHOOL ————————

Robert ("Rocky") Rock, a social studies teacher, developed a role-based unit on invention and creative problem solving for a seventh-and-eighth-grade class. The unit actually built on a prior set of lessons in which the students researched the history and construction of various inventions, such as televisions, bicycles, and toasters. This prior unit culminated in the students' producing posters that described their findings for each invention. The new, role-based activity was designed so that for some of these inventions the groups would ultimately come up with possible improvements based on ideas suggested by four roles: environmentalist, scientist, engineer, and consumer.

Rocky started his students out with a thorough exploration of each of the four roles. The class was divided into groups of four students each, with each group member taking a different role so that all four were represented in each group. The students then spent a couple of lessons exploring the fine points of their roles—checking definitions in the dictionary, looking up further information about the role when possible, answering questions about the role (such as "What hobbies or interests do you associate with this role?"), and even attending a brief "convention" with the other class members researching the same role to discuss and firm up their understanding of what the role involved. Indeed, many teachers with whom we have worked concur in stressing the importance of helping students express and develop their knowledge of an academic role before proceeding to apply the role.

The next phase of this unit was for the students in their original groups to envision improvements in their assigned invention that would appeal to all four role perspectives. Finally, each group created and presented an advertisement for their improved invention. Most of these commercials took the form of skits, which the teacher videotaped.

One further step that would carry the role applications fully into the students' lives outside school would be to ask the groups to use the same roles to help them come up with feasible improvements for something they actually could change. For instance, they might figure out how the four roles would suggest improving plans for a party or ways to improve relations with a friend or family member. Or they might simply come up with an improved actual invention, such as a new version of a game they play or a new kind of decoration for bicycles. The message would be that the new ways of thinking they learn in school can be usefully applied in many ways in their lives right now.

## AN EXAMPLE FROM HIGH SCHOOL

Fletch Coolidge, a high school science teacher, has developed a way to orient his students toward applying any subject they study to any issue they choose. He starts out by asking the class (working in small groups) to list major problems in the world and in their lives. The class then narrows the list to the ten issues most frequently mentioned among all groups. Working again in groups, the students next brainstorm ways that the science topic of the week (such as weather) could help illuminate or solve the problems. Overpopulation, for example, could be controlled by natural disasters; rain and mud would slow down tanks in a war; and so on. The whole class then discusses and shares the groups' ideas.

During the next class the students choose other academic areas and discuss how the science topic is important in each of these domains—areas such as home economics, shop, history, and health. Then in their groups the class returns to the original top ten problems to consider how these other academic disciplines might help solve the problems. How, for example, could home economics help solve problems related to war? Could the idea that "an army travels on its stomach" be a clue? Groups then share their ideas.

Finally, for "home fun" students are asked to consider with their families what they can do to help deal with the problems the class has been considering. Fletch sees his efforts as a way of encouraging—and empowering—students to use all their subjects as starting points for dealing with a wide variety of real concerns in their lives and in the world at large.

**NOTES**

## Thinking up New Purposes

Before we reach the special creativity-enhancing awareness plans, let's pause to consider that not only problem solving but also problem or goal *generation* is essential to creative functioning in life. Getzels and Csikszentmihalyi (1976), in their research on artistic creativity, discovered that *problem finding* is an important aspect of originality. Young artists who spent much time surveying a situation and exploring new perspectives and possibilities for their art produced more exciting work than those who devoted the same time to carefully developing their first ideas. Similarly, great inventions may result more often from seeing a new problem than from coming up with a solution to an old one. And back in the mundane world, we have found that a key difficulty for students learning to use meta-thinking is the strain of thinking up goals to work on. The upshot: Self-direction and creativity would be enhanced if people could come up with meaningful new purposes more easily.

How might academic roles and content help out? The most direct route could be to ask what advice people in different subject-area roles would offer for new goals or problems. Students taking on the geographer role, for instance, might suggest various types of travel or exploration. This could range from goals such as visiting new places to exploring new "regions" of experience—say, through meditation, reading, or conversation. Taking the role of an economist might suggest looking for activities that earn higher "interest" in the form of emotional well-being. Historical thinking might lead to new goals for "revolution" in troublesome areas of one's life or to using aspects of the past to suggest new things to strive for now. The role of an artist could prompt ideas for new forms of personal expression or searching for beauty in unlikely places. The output from use of the Wealth AP (see chapter 6) can also serve to suggest new purposes to pursue. The new meanings for wealth suggested by any academic domain can provide excellent starting places.

Why not try out some of this for yourself right now? Take a few of your favorite subjects, literary authors (or characters), or specific topics you teach and list a few goals or purposes that each one suggests to you. If even one of these goals strikes your fancy and gives you some new ideas about possible purposes in life, this little exercise should be well worth the time.

This approach can open anyone's mind to a wide array of possible purposes. And it is very easy to integrate with practically any lesson or subject area. All you need do is pose the question "What new personal goals does this content suggest for you?" and then give the students a chance to answer, perhaps in a free-write (a period of writing without stopping, with no concern for spelling or punctuation) or in a brief class discussion.

## Using Academic Subjects to Enhance Creativity

There are many rules of thumb (sometimes referred to as "heuristics") for boosting creativity. Most of these are in fact awareness plans intended to spark new and useful ideas for solving problems. For this chapter we have culled a representative sample of approaches that seem especially effective. We examine how each of these creativity enhancers can be used to increase the power of using academic roles to help with problem solving. Our list begins with our old favorite, role-taking itself.

**NOTES**

### Role-Taking

A good way to cultivate creative thinking is to try out new perspectives, new ways of looking at things. Probably the single most accessible and powerful way to do this is to think of various roles and then mentally put yourself in each one. Indeed, *any* awareness plan can be couched as a role. Simply say to yourself, "Try thinking like someone who . . . thinks of holiday themes for each day, or looks for points in other people's ideas to build on, or asks questions about everything, or uses different roles as an aid for problem solving, or constantly applies academic content to enrich life, or _____" (fill in with any AP you choose). Perhaps because role-playing is associated with fun, entertainment, and drama, it is often easier to employ a new awareness plan by thinking of it as playing a role rather than as directing your thoughts.

Indeed, this and later chapters show how roles (thought patterns) derived from academic specialties can be used to boost one's creativity in using other awareness plans—awareness plans designed to enrich life in the various ways discussed in this book. Thus, most of this book can be regarded as a set of illustrations for how to use the role-taking creativity plan for the purpose of applying academic content to enrich life.

However, in addition to asking how a particular specialist role would advise you to use a particular AP or solve a particular problem, you can use the specialist role to suggest other possible roles. For instance, a mathematician might suggest the roles of subspecialists (such as topologist or specialist in arithmetic or algebra) or, more playfully, such roles as imagined personifications of infinity, the null set, or the number 13. From the master role of film specialist, you might derive further roles such as particular directors, actors, or film characters (or even zanier roles such as personified projectors or screens). What subsidiary roles do each of the following master roles bring to mind?

**Biologist:**

**Historian:**

**Poet:**

**Economist:**

**Astronomer:**

**Artist:**

(Reminder—In any of our exercises, *please feel free to substitute roles based on your own areas of interest or teaching* for the sample roles we suggest.)

Of course, drawing on academic roles to suggest subsidiary roles is only a first step. The next move would be to use the suggested roles to generate new ideas for whatever you were striving to do more creatively. And this brings us to a crucial aside about the use of role taking and most other creativity plans.

---

### *Crucial Aside: Dancing the Two-Step*

**Most creativity plans have at least two steps.**

**The first step** (*new* ideas) is generally to shake up your thinking in some way. You can do this by trying on new roles, using new metaphors, reversing your goals or ideas, breaking a problem into subproblems, free associating to random words drawn from the dictionary, meditating, or anything else that works for you.

**The second step** (*good* ideas) is to build on the ideas generated in the first step. Sometimes your initial ideas will solve your problem or give you an effective innovation without further elaboration, but if you are truly using a creativity plan to generate new starting places, the first step will normally yield just that—new *starting* places. ***Don't stop at a starting place!*** (Another bumper sticker?) Those often strange, apparently useless notions that many creativity provokers help you generate may catapult you to exciting new solutions when you build on them.

Now back to our discussion.

Here is a simple example of how the two-step process can work in relation to the role-taking plan. Let's say two friends want to use roles to generate new ideas for resolving a conflict. Starting with the master role of artist, they might decide to try such subroles as painter (or a specific painter, such as Picasso), sculptor, potter, or whatever. This is part of the shake-up, or new-starting-point stage. Then they might build on the role of painter to generate ideas such as drawing pictures of their conflict as a way to initiate new insights and a possible resolution. (Using the Picasso role might lead to further ideas, such as deliberately drawing the conflict in distorted ways or using many different perspectives.)

Notice, though, that genuine solutions will call for step two—building on the ideas generated by the initial subroles. In our example, for instance, the fighting friends could discuss their drawings and build on any insights the drawings yield in order to work out agreeable resolutions to their problems. Or they might call on still other roles to help refine the painter's suggestions. The role of historian, say, might lead them to try drawing a series of pictures tracing the events leading up to their spat—and perhaps also drawing how they might resolve the problem in the future.

The creativity plans that follow demonstrate further how this mental "two-step" dance unfolds in practice.

### Breaking Down

No, we're not referring to going off the deep end or even to weeping in frustration at a tough creativity challenge. This plan is actually our most logical and conventionally sane approach. It is to subdivide any problem or goal into smaller components.

Generally, this division is easy to do without extra creativity assistance, but sometimes it can help a lot to get a new slant on just *how* to break a challenging goal or situation into subparts. It is at such times that academic roles can come in handy. Each subject-derived role can lead to new ways to analyze a goal or problem. Let's say students want to boost their self-confidence. Taking the role of an economist might suggest doing a kind of cost-benefit analysis, dividing the problem into "cost" areas where students want to reduce difficulties (things that drag down their self-confidence) and "benefit" areas where they want to enhance things that boost their confidence. Historical thinking, on the other hand, might lead students to break their goals into temporal components (such as the steps in developing new skills) or the amount of time each component might take. Biology might suggest looking at self-confidence in terms of relevance to health or survival (such as various types of physical self-confidence) or drawing analogies between the problem and organic structures or functions (for example, the "nucleus" of the problem versus its "cytoplasm" and "cellular membrane").

What categories for breaking down this or other goals and problems might be suggested by the roles of

**NOTES**

**short-story writer**

**nutritionist**

**sports analyst**

**or expert in your favorite subject?**

**NOTES**

Once you have selected a scheme for decomposing your goal or problem, you of course still need to formulate and examine the actual subgoals or subproblems. But notice that all this is but the first step in using the break-down plan. The big second step is to try figuring out some solutions for each subproblem. Otherwise all you're left with is a list of new problems. The other creativity plans discussed in this chapter can readily be used in tandem with the break-down approach to help generate actual solutions for the subproblems or subgoals.

### Reversing Goals or Ideas

All right, enough sanity and logic for now; it's time to get a little wacky. How about *reversing* your goal and then using academic roles to help figure out how to work toward the reversed goal? (Stay calm; the second step in this plan will be to build on—or perhaps to re-reverse—these perverse ideas to generate something really useful.)

First, why should reversing your goal be a good approach at all? For one thing, it is a way to shake up your thinking. Usually we focus on how to solve problems or get what we think we want, so switching to figuring out how to undo solutions or make problems worse or get what we think we don't want will at least be something new to do with our minds— and hence potentially useful for step one.

But reversing goals can do more than just gyrate our minds. It often is easier to come up with ideas for how to make something worse than for how to improve it. In a psychological research study conducted some years ago (see Leff, Gordon, and Ferguson 1974), college students were asked to imagine either how to improve a scene or how to make it worse. Although the students generally reported enjoying imagining improvements more than the reverse, raters judged the students' reported ideas and images for making the scene worse to be more creative than the ideas and images for improving the scene. A possible reason for this effect could be that people have a bigger store of negative images and possibilities than of positive ones. This could result from a common human tendency to be more alert to possible trouble than to possible benefits. Or perhaps it is simply easier to foul things up than to make them better. In any case, if reverse thinking sparks creativity, why not take advantage of it?

Taking advantage of ideas about how to make something worse, though, calls for its own brand of creative thinking. The upshot, nicely fitting the theme of this book, is that academic content and roles can help out both for thinking creatively in reverse and for building constructively on whatever strange starting places the reversed thinking yields. Let us demonstrate with an example.

## Example

Your goal is to enjoy reading an assigned dull book. Reversing this, you first figure out ways to make the reading less enjoyable. (This is, of course, step one.) To give yourself some new ideas for how to do this, you draw on the academic role of geographer, let's say. What comes to mind?

**Some of our ideas:** Look for very uncomfortable places. Seek "resources" that work against enjoying reading, such as noise, crowds, lack of food, poor lighting, negative thoughts about the book, distractions, and so on. Stir guilt feelings by imagining your culture regards reading your book as taboo. Think about the natural resources being wasted on production of the book. Remind yourself about the lack of geographically interesting pictures or information in the book.

Now you build on your ideas to come up with constructive possibilities for your original goal, again drawing on an academic role to help out your creativity. (You are now entering step two—the generation of potential solutions or good ideas.) You can stay with the original role or try new ones for this phase of the process. Let's say you switch to a scientist role for this round. What ideas does that generate for building on the "reversed" geographical thinking in step one?

**Some examples:** Look for places to read that are comfortable for some "chemical" reason—perhaps because of pleasant aromas or a special "bond" between you and the surroundings. Amass positive resources that make use of modern scientific advances, such as white noise generators to mask environmental distractions, high-tech tasty food, daylight-spectrum lighting, positive awareness plans about the book based on psychological research, and so on. Think about cultures in which reading your book could contribute to scientific advances of some kind and make you feel proud. Think of how efficiently your book is using resources to convey information and how many scientific advances have gone into printing. Remind yourself about these scientific wonders as you read and about how they add to the interest of whatever is in the book.

Now, using any academic role(s) of your choice, what are some further suggestions for making dull reading even worse—and then for building on these negative ideas to suggest ways to make dull reading more interesting?

## Asking "What If . . . ?"

Another extremely powerful two-step aid to creativity is to jog your thinking first by contemplating what would happen if the world (or at least your problem situation) were somehow very different. Then, for step two, you build on these "counterfactual" ideas (which provide strange new starting places for your thought) to generate promising possible solutions. Both steps, once again, offer excellent pathways for using academic content and roles to grease the wheels of your mind.

Let's jump right into an example to show how this process can work.

## Example

Let's say your goal is to redesign your classroom creatively for very little money.

**Note:** You may find yourself already thinking up solutions. Actually, that's normal. Indeed, if you come up with satisfying solutions to any problem without deliberately using creativity plans, go for it. Why expend extra energy if your mind supplies ready answers without assistance? However, if you want still more possibilities, or if you get stuck, this and the other plans can provide real help. At least for this example, pretend that you desperately want to generate some new possibilities and are willing to try an offbeat approach.

The first part of the first step for "What if-ing" is to pose some strange, hypothetical questions about either your classroom or its context. For instance, you might ask, "What if everyone in the class were blind?" "What if we all had to live in this classroom permanently?" "What if this were a one-room schoolhouse?" "What if education operated as a religion?" STOP! Okay, now to enhance thinking up new what if's, let's bring in some academic roles. Add your own counterfactual questions for each role.

*Mathematician:*

**What if the room were a sphere?**

**What if the dimensions were all multiplied by 3?**

*Historian:*

**What if your room were in various other times (such as 1944 or the early 1800s)?**

**What if the original Inca culture dominated our society?**

*Economist:*

**What if we lived in a barter economy?**

**What if your room had to be changed so that it took in money somehow?**

As you would guess, the next step is the second step. Here you build on the ideas from step one to form creative, workable, real possibilities for your original goal (in this example, redesigning your classroom). Once again, though, academic roles can be used to facilitate the process. How, for instance, might different types of scientists build on the barter economy notion or the room-has-to-make-money idea to suggest new room designs?

For example, geologist: ask students to bring in interesting rocks to display and to trade with each other; physicist: set up a class light-and-sound show, and for admission ask visitors to bring something with unusual physical properties to decorate the room.

Or what innovative ideas does a role based on the work of your favorite novelist suggest from the Inca what if? (This may take some thought, but you might surprise yourself with the ideas you generate.)

Remember, creativity plans are intended ultimately to generate actual solutions, not just unusual ideas or odd starting places. Human thought is very good at forming connections, however. Just be sure to direct your mind to link the unusual starting place to the goal! (Which brings us to our next plan . . . )

## *Forming Unusual Connections*

A very powerful way to use academic roles to inspire creative thinking is to employ them to make deliberately odd connections with your goal. One effective path is to start by asking what *absurd* ideas a variety of specialists might suggest for a goal of yours. The second step would be to use other specialist roles to help you connect those absurd ideas to useful solutions. For instance, a geologist might suggest treating an unruly class to a "volcanic eruption" of yelling and throwing things at the students. To build constructively on that wild idea, a French specialist might suggest "erupting" in a foreign language (which could be extended, using other roles, to "languages" such as music, drawing, poetry, or whatever strikes your fancy). The final result could be a humorous, instructive, and effective way to gain a class's attention.

A slightly more serious way to use academic roles and content to foster unusual connections is to select concepts from a subject area and then figure out links with your goal. Step two in this case would be to use the same or other academic roles to suggest possible solutions based on these unusual links. Say you start with the same unruly class and look for links from the field of meteorology, such as various types of storms or clouds. One link might be to see your class's behavior as a kind of "atmospheric disturbance" in their usual behavior patterns. This, in turn, might suggest possible "meteorological" solutions such as issuing "storm warnings" to the class, rating their behavior—in good humor—on the scale of hurricane intensity ("Force 1" to "Force 5"), humorously barricading yourself, or perhaps spinning the kids off to separate locales to "break up the storm." Alternatively, you might ask how, say, a philosopher or an artist might build on the storm analogy. This could in turn suggest possibilities such as asking the students to debate the ethics of "behavioral storms" or to draw pictures of their "churned up" feelings.

**NOTES**

## Still More Creativity Plans

Here, in brief form, are some other ways to "power up" creative thinking—and to use academic subject areas to facilitate creativity.

- **Try new metaphors for your goal or problem situation.** This approach was just illustrated in the meteorology example for the "unusual connections" plan. As discussed further in chapter 3, thinking up new metaphors automatically generates new connections and new perspectives. Academic content, with its vast and intricate array of new concepts, offers a striking resource for drawing out new metaphors. We can, for instance, think of an unruly class not only as a behavioral storm, but as a catalyst or acid (chemistry), a dissonant chord or an orchestra tuning up (music), or even the cube root of a revolution (math and history)—and each new metaphor can suggest new ideas for dealing with the problem. What solutions would you derive from these or other metaphors for an unruly class?

- **Think of situations and activities that contribute to your creativity.** Simply thinking about what helps you to be creative can often put you in a more creative mood. Even better, of course, is actually doing something to re-create those conditions. At the very least try vividly imagining that you are doing whatever it is (or are located wherever it is) that seems to help your creativity. And to jog further ideas about what might evoke your creative thinking, try turning to imagined subject-area advisers for some ideas. What, for example, might a nuclear physicist or a medieval historian suggest that could contribute to your creativity?

(We think of splitting or fusing our ideas, looking for a critical mass of knowledge or creativity plans, then of sitting quietly in a sanctuary to meditate on a problem or goal, or going on a crusade to "convert" others to help us generate new ideas.)

- **Pretend you have a magic wand that frees you to break your assumptions of feasibility.** The essence of this plan is to trick yourself into laying aside your concerns about practicality and feasibility by making wishes. Then you can build on these fanciful ideas by noticing what features of your wishes hold special appeal and figuring out things you could do that would embody those aspects. Academic roles and content can contribute both by providing ideas for new wishes and by aiding in deriving practical ideas from the wishes. For instance, what might a health specialist wish for to improve faculty meetings?

(Perhaps turning them into magical stress-reduction sessions, or into periods of rejuvenating exercise for both body and mind?)

Then, how might different fields suggest building realistically on these wishes?

(For example, language arts: use meetings to compose and share free-writings on sources of stress in school—and on ideas for alleviation; geology: plan faculty meetings as forums for progressively eroding sources of stress—say, by picking out one small stress-related problem to solve during each meeting.)

- **Invent games that spin off creative ideas as they are played.** This approach is a little complicated, but it can be both very effective and a lot of fun. It works best with a group of people. The basic process is to formulate some kind of gamelike procedure that requires all players to generate new ideas for solving the problem. For instance, you might try a "Can You Top This?" approach, whereby each person in turn must offer an improvement on the previous person's idea (perhaps drawing on academic roles or content to do so). Academic content can enter both by suggesting new game procedures (see the Game Plan in chapter 3) and by helping each player generate creative ideas as the game is played.

**Note:** Cooperative game structures, where players build on each other's ideas and work collaboratively, are generally most helpful for boosting creativity; see chapter 8.

- **Look for good points in other people's ideas, and try building on an idea before criticizing it.** Next to role-taking, this is our favorite process for boosting creativity. This constructive approach to other people's ideas helps not only to boost your own creativity but also to create a productive and cooperative social atmosphere (see Stein 1974, 162–68; Prince 1970). In effect, it boosts everyone's creativity. Academic subject areas and roles can also contribute very handily to being more effective in actually building on others' ideas. The general boost to creativity provided by academic role "advice" is especially useful for building on apparently off-track or flawed ideas. Simply ask, "How might _____ (an anthropologist, a character in a novel, or whatever) suggest building on this idea?" (See chapters 5 and 7 for further discussion and examples of this process.)

**NOTES**

## Sample Lesson Plan

Here is an example of a general lesson plan structure for using academic content to nurture creative thinking about matters that matter to students.

**GOAL:** To use subject matter and academic thought patterns to boost creative thinking

**SAMPLE PROCEDURE:**

*Step 1:* Ask the class to brainstorm problems or goals about which they would like to think more creatively. These could be personal issues, social problems, academic problems, things that are going well that they would like to improve further, or even some problems from the subject matter they are studying. Make sure the issues are listed for all to see.

*Step 2:* Get the students to form groups based on their favorite problem or goal from the list. Also assign each group another problem from the list as a second issue (see step 4 for how this second problem will be treated).

*Step 3:* Ask each group to work together on their chosen problem, generating ideas by using several different roles based on current subject matter they are studying. (All of the roles can be drawn from a single subject area if you like.)

**Note:** We assume you will have already explained how to use academic roles. Also, either in the initial activity or as a follow-up, give students specific creativity plans discussed in this chapter to go along with the academic roles. It is important for each group to use several roles, however.

*Step 4:* Ask each group now to work on the second, assigned issue, using the academic role (and any associated creativity plan) that helped the group generate its most promising idea for the problem it chose.

*Step 5:* Give each group a chance to share its favorite ideas for both its chosen and assigned issues and to tell how the group used academic roles and creativity plans to generate these ideas.

*Step 6:* Ask each student to free-write on what she or he learned from the activity—including learning about how to use the subject matter, about group processes, and about creative thinking.

**EVALUATION:** The students' group reports and free-writing can be assessed for relevance to the learning goals of the curricular content. In addition, the reports and free-writing can be used to evaluate possible gains in creative thinking, ability to use subject content and roles, group process skills, and even solutions for the real-life issues the groups tackled.

**FOLLOW-UP:** Students can be asked to report, either in journals or in class discussion, on any actual use they make of the ideas and processes explored in the activity. Of course, a powerful in-class follow-up would be to do similar problem-generating and problem-solving activities, using more of the creativity plans presented in this chapter (or in the suggested readings). It is also very useful to encourage students to use a wider and wider range of subject-area roles and content to assist in their problem solving both in and out of school. You might also encourage them to share their newly learned problem-solving skills with people outside the class (outreach).

What other follow-up ideas can you think of right now? What might various creativity plans and academic roles suggest? See if you can envision an activity or assignment based on each of the creativity-evoking awareness plans from this chapter (see summary figure).

# Summary Awareness Plan Map

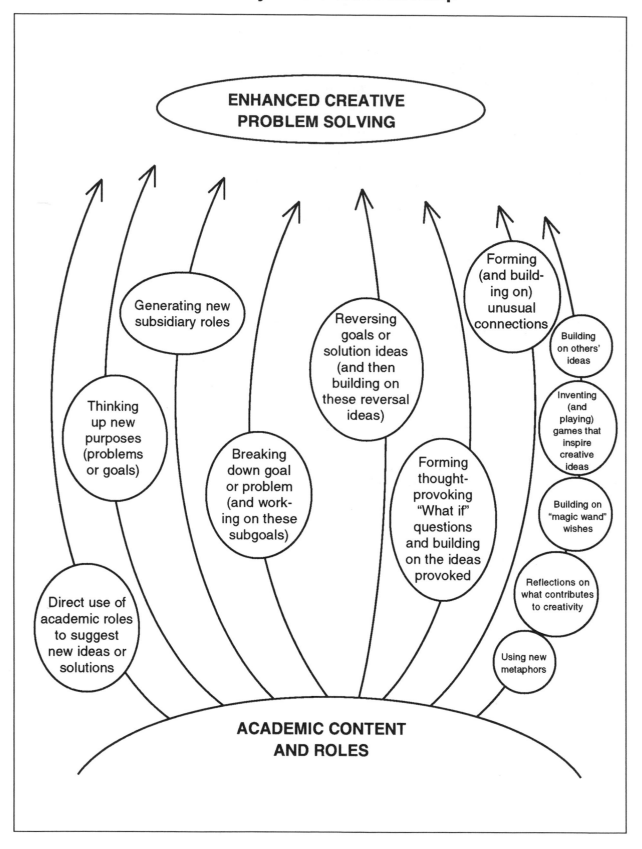

## Suggested Readings on Creativity and Its Enhancement

Adams, James L. *Conceptual Blockbusting*. Reading, Mass.: Addison-Wesley, 1986.
Clear, applied ideas for understanding and overcoming blocks to creative thinking.

Amabile, Teresa M. *The Social Psychology of Creativity*. New York: Springer-Verlag, 1983.
Rich, detailed account of the role of intrinsic motivation in supporting creativity.

——. *Growing up Creative*. New York: Crown, 1989.
Popularly written update of intrinsic motivation principle and research, with useful tips for applications in education and child rearing.

Arieti, Silvano. *Creativity: The Magic Synthesis*. New York: Basic Books, 1976.
Thought-provoking theory of creativity stressing the role of subconscious processes and the importance of social and cultural context.

Barron, Frank. *Creativity and Personal Freedom*. Princeton, N.J.: Van Nostrand, 1968.
Classic account of personality traits associated with creativity.

Capacchione, Lucia. *The Creative Journal*. Athens, Ohio: Ohio University Press, 1979.
Highly interactive workbook approach to using visual thinking and expression for self-exploration and creativity enhancement.

de Bono, Edward. *The Mechanism of Mind*. New York: Simon & Schuster, 1969.
Presentation of de Bono's underlying theory of mental processes and creativity.

——. *Lateral Thinking: Creativity Step by Step*. New York: Harper & Row, 1970.
Classic presentation of key approach and supporting techniques developed by this superstar in the field of creativity education.

——. *Six Thinking Hats*. Boston: Little, Brown, 1985.
Update of de Bono's ideas on stimulating creativity, incorporating multiple modes of thinking (including a meta-mode).

Edwards, Betty. *Drawing on the Artist Within*. New York: Simon & Schuster, 1986.
Very helpfully illustrated approach to using drawing to represent and solve problems creatively.

Finke, Ronald A., Thomas B. Ward, and Steven M. Smith. *Creative Cognition: Theory, Research, and Applications*. Cambridge, Mass.: The MIT Press, 1992.
Detailed account of these authors' recent theory and research emphasizing a two-level process in creative invention.

Gardner, Howard. *Frames of Mind: The Theory of Multiple Intelligences*. New York: Basic Books, 1983.
Highly readable discussion of seven kinds of intelligence; very helpful for extending our conception of types of mental abilities.

——. *Multiple Intelligences: The Theory in Practice*. New York: Basic Books, 1993a.
Wide-ranging update on educational applications (and implications) of the theory of multiple intelligences.

——. *Creating Minds: An Anatomy of Creativity Seen through the Lives of Freud, Einstein, Picasso, Stravinsky, Eliot, Graham, and Gandhi*. New York: Basic Books, 1993b.
Fascinating analysis of the multifaceted nature of extraordinary creativity, clearly intertwining Gardner's theory with these impressive case histories.

Gordon, William J. J. *Synectics: The Development of Creative Capacity.* New York: Macmillan, 1961.

> Classic account of this highly effective approach to facilitating group (and individual) creative thinking.

——. *The Metaphorical Way of Learning and Knowing.* Cambridge, Mass.: Porpoise Books, 1973.

> Application of synectics techniques to educational practice.

Koberg, Don, and Jim Bagnall. *The Universal Traveler* (New Horizons ed.). Los Altos, Calif.: Crisp Publications, 1991.

> Compendium of useful and diverse techniques for enhancing creative problem solving, organized around a journey metaphor.

Koestler, Arthur. *The Act of Creation.* New York: Dell, 1964.

> Classic account of Koestler's theory that creativity arises from the process of "bisociation": the union of diverse frames of reference.

Lakoff, George, and Mark Johnson. *Metaphors We Live By.* Chicago: University of Chicago Press, 1980.

> Profound look at how metaphorical thinking—understanding and experiencing something in terms of something else—serves human thought and creativity.

Leff, Herbert L. *Playful Perception: Choosing How to Experience Your World.* Burlington, Vt.: Waterfront Books, 1984.

> Photographically illustrated sampling of a wide range of creativity-enhancing awareness plans.

Perkins, David N. *The Mind's Best Work.* Cambridge, Mass.: Harvard University Press, 1981.

> Clearly argued theory that creative thinking is basically effective thinking.

Prince, George M. *The Practice of Creativity.* New York: Macmillan, 1970.

> Another classic in synectics, or metaphorical thinking, focusing on the rationale and specific techniques for using this very empowering approach to facilitating creative thinking in groups.

Stein, Morris I. *Stimulating Creativity.* New York: Academic Press, 1974, 1975.

> A two-volume compendium on theory and research concerning the facilitation of both individual and group creativity.

Vaughan, Frances E. *Awakening Intuition.* New York: Doubleday, 1979.

> A very readable guide to using mental imagery to assist in self-understanding and creativity.

von Oech, Roger. *A Kick in the Seat of the Pants.* New York: Harper and Row, 1986.

> An exploration of four key general "roles" involved in creative thinking and problem solving.

——. *A Whack on the Side of the Head.* 2nd ed. New York: Warner Books, 1990.

> A humorous, offbeat presentation of several dozen ways to overcome various "mental locks" that block creativity.

See also *The Journal of Creative Behavior,* published by the Creative Education Foundation, Buffalo, New York; and *Creativity Research Journal,* published by Ablex Publishing Corporation, Norwood, New Jersey.

# 3

# Learning for Playfulness

What is at the heart of *playfulness?* What are key principles for encouraging its development? How can academic content be used to enhance playful ways of thinking? How can we structure educational activities to embody these principles and ways of thinking?

## Principles of Playfulness

We believe that at the heart (and the art) of playfulness lies the tendency to explore, to try out new approaches, to make new connections, and to sprinkle a touch of humor, lightness, and even zaniness through whatever one is up to. Of course, when people think playfully, the results can be seriously important; just witness the scientific breakthroughs, inventions, literature, and other good ideas that have been spawned by playful thinking. In addition to such useful spinoffs, however, playfulness also turns out an unmistakably immediate benefit: fun.

Over the past several years we have proposed some "principles of playfulness," intended as a set of guidelines for encouraging playful thinking (see Leff 1986; Nevin and Leff 1990). Here is a summary:

**NOTES**

1. **Power**. Playfulness works. It increases creativity, intrinsic satisfaction, and zest for life and thought. Understanding this power makes it easier to play by reducing our cultural bias that "play is frivolous" (see also von Oech 1990).

2. **Permission**. Playfulness flourishes when you and the people around you say it's okay to play. Often this okay is all it takes to call forth a blooming bouquet of creative play from people who least expect it of themselves.

3. **Proaction**. Playfulness can be facilitated by deliberately selecting awareness plans that give you a nudge toward fresh and sometimes zany ways of thinking.

4. **Practice**. The more you consciously, pro-actively engage in playful thinking, the more capable (and spontaneous) you become at being playful.

5. **Proliferation**. The more widely you infuse playfulness into your life and the more you invite and help others to do the same, the easier and richer playfulness becomes. Also, in general, two can play better than one.

## Using Academic Subjects Playfully

Now, for the main course of this chapter, let's dig into some awareness plans cooked up especially to nourish mental playfulness. Naturally, we will be sampling academically spiced-up versions of these plans—and suggestions for how to lay out a full educational feast for your students.

### The Holiday Plan

What if we thought of each day as a special holiday of some sort? The awareness plan underlying this question—thinking of each day as a holiday—has proven very buoying to us personally and to a number of our students. In fact, we have seen this particular

AP generated anew on several occasions, such as a group of college students grappling with the problem of energizing themselves to get up early in the morning. They ultimately settled on this awareness plan as their favorite solution.

The trick in using the Holiday AP lies, in part, in what specific sort of holiday you envision the day to be. "Outrageous Clothes Day," for instance, might lead you to dress outrageously or at least to pay special attention to any unusual attire you notice on other people (inwardly congratulating yourself for each outrageous item of clothing you notice). "Transportation Day" could lead you to relish any form of travel and perhaps to make a point of using as many different modes of transit as you can during the day. "Humor Day" might suggest you search out new jokes everywhere you can, or perhaps try making up something funny about every situation you encounter. Clearly, each possible holiday theme excites some corresponding awareness and behavior plan ideas, and carrying through on them can be fun.

Part of the trick, though, is simply thinking of the day as a holiday, regardless of the specific theme. A holiday is something special, something calling for celebration and energy. Actually, this general connotation of "specialness" combines with the specific theme to provide an energizing direction or focus for the day. And with a little thought, it is possible to make every day unique, interesting, and, if you like, playful. (Indeed, you might try listing some especially playful possible holiday themes right now, such as "Toy Day," "Crazy Ideas Day," "Surprise Day," or "Inside-Out Day.")

One of our favorite features of this AP is how easy—and how appropriate—it is to enrich it with academic content. All you need to do is plug in a subject area or concept as the holiday theme. What types of special activities and awareness plans come to mind for each of the following holidays?

## HISTORY DAY

## MULTIPLICATION DAY

## GEOGRAPHY DAY
(easily multiplied into Africa Day, Cities Day, Explorer Day, Map Day, and so on)

**BIOLOGY DAY**

_____ **DAY**

(your favorite subject)

_____ **DAY**

(your least favorite specific topic)

Now that you have envisioned a whole holiday based on your least favorite topic, what are some new possibilities for how to approach this topic?

The real fun may derive most from thinking up—and actually carrying out—playful, creative things to do based on the holiday theme. The "Explorer Day" theme, for instance, might suggest picking out actual explorers and using something about their exploits to generate an interesting exploration of your own. Thus, "Sacajawea Day" might lead to a wilderness outing, if possible, or to guiding a friend to some of one's favorite spots. Or in following up on "Entropy Day," students might suggest a scavenger hunt for things that best represent processes of entropy and negentropy, or perhaps the day could be taken as a challenge to restore order to something that is falling into disarray.

Perhaps more clearly than any other AP we have encountered, the Holiday Plan demonstrates the power and value of academic enhancement of awareness plans. First, the conceptual richness of academic subject matter clearly helps to generate an endless stream of new ideas for holiday themes, thus beautifully illustrating the power of scholastic content to provide our minds with new starting points. In addition, creators and users of academically amplified versions of the Holiday Plan will readily see that the richer their actual knowledge of the subject area is, the more interesting and useful will be their ideas both for holiday themes and for follow-through activities.

The Holiday Plan is actually part of a family of playful APs. Before introducing the parent of that family (a true meta-plan), let's take a peek at a few of the other offspring.

## The Game Plan

The essence of this awareness plan is to think of whatever is going on as a game or to figure out how to make it into a game. This approach is actually very natural for many people, especially in boring, repetitive, or taxing situations. Co-workers may make a friendly race out of a joint task, for instance, or travelers might challenge themselves to spot various types of objects on a long trip. Can you think of a time when you have made something dull or difficult into a game? What did you do? How did your thinking and feeling change?

A somewhat more "psychological" use of the Game Plan is to regard whatever you or other people are doing as a game and then to guess what the rules are and perhaps to supply a game name that fits. We have used this approach on occasion during slow-moving meetings, for example. First imagining that we are novices and all other participants are seasoned players, we then try to figure out what the rules of the game are and what constitutes good plays. A meeting might then be seen, say, as a contest to win attention or respect or maybe as the "Put 'Em to Sleep" game or, more positively, as a cooperative idea-building game. Most generally, you can even use the Game AP to reinterpret virtually anything you or others do as some kind of implicit game. Some popular psychology books (especially those about transactional analysis) have provided examples of this reinterpretation, but a simple approach is just to name any activity as a game and then follow up by thinking about what the rules and good playing techniques are. What comes to mind for

## the Conversation Game?

## the Teaching Game?

## the Eating Game?

**the Dreaming Game?**

[writing box]

To integrate with the first version of the Game Plan, you might also think of ways to make each of these "games" more genuinely playful and fun.

[writing box]

To use academic content to enrich the Game AP, we can rephrase the plan as follows: Think of how you can regard or turn _____ (whatever situation or activity you pick) into a game based on _____ (whatever academic field, ideas, or thought patterns you select). For example, what sorts of math games might you make out of washing dishes?

[writing box]

How might a daily commute be regarded as a history game of some sort?
(Perhaps by looking for changes each day, or . . . ?)

How many different geography games or biology games can you
think up for watching TV?

New possibilities for playful academic enrichments of everyday experience are surprisingly easy to generate when the Game Plan is called into play. A clever example of a game structure based on academic subject matter was recently suggested by one of our students. She faced the problem of getting her housemates to help out with tasks such as washing the dishes. Her solution was a game in which each person would roll a die to determine which of six roles to play while doing the task. The roles our student chose were based on material from a college course in social psychology (such as "discriminator" so that one might, say, be especially rough in scrubbing cups but gentle with plates, or "arbitrator" whereby one's job might be to settle disputes about who is to do a particular batch of dishes). The beauty of this game structure is that *any* academic field can contribute roles, and any task can be approached with a playful spirit based on the roles. For instance, students might add zest to studying by first generating roles based on a subject and then randomly selecting one of these roles to play while doing homework. History, for example, might suggest roles such as dictator, revolutionary, inventor, and journalist. Biology might generate roles such as virus, predator, bee, and root. Each of these roles, in turn, could lead to some entertaining—and productive—new approaches to studying. What are a few roles based on something you teach, and how might these roles be used in this game format? (Challenge yourself to be especially playful with this one.)

## The Adventure Plan

A sibling of the Game and Holiday APs is a game in which you view whatever you are up to as an adventure of some sort. What goes into an adventure?

Our answer: a sense of anticipation, excitement, uncertainty, risk, need for vigilance, and perhaps a story line (see also the Story Plan later in this chapter).

To turn any situation into an adventure, you need to read significance into whatever is happening. What if your life were part of a novel or a movie being filmed? What adventurous themes might underlie what you are doing today?

In reading this book right now, for instance, you might see yourself as an explorer of strange and possibly dangerous new ways to use your mind and to lead your tribe (students) into new domains of thought. Even simple acts such as brushing your teeth might be taken as an adventure in flushing out invading food particles and sneaking up on the ever-lurking, invisible plaque bacteria. And just think what you can do with complex events such as teaching a class, correcting student work, or meeting with parents!

Academic Enhancement: View _____ (whatever you choose) as an adventure based on themes derived from _____ (any academic field you pick). For instance, cleaning the house might become a biological adventure in several ways—hunting bugs or spider webs, protecting the health of yourself or your family in various ways informed by biological knowledge, treating the whole cleaning process as an elaborate form of adventurous new physical exercise (and perhaps finding new ways to clean to enhance the exercise value). Or talking with a student's parents might become a geographical adventure by exploring with them various "regions" and "resources" of the student's life (or even just places the student has lived or visited)—or perhaps by viewing the conversation itself as movement through a "relationship space" involving you, the parents, and the student; what strange terrain might you encounter?

Of course, these examples are rather tame as adventures go. How about some real adventures based on academic subject matter? Two extremely creative teachers we know, Diane Happy and Karen Pearo, had groups in their combined first-and-second-grade class use themes from classroom readings to devise fun-house style cardboard constructions through which each team led the rest of the class in a real experiential adventure. This approach can be extended readily to any grade and subject by suggesting that students create adventurous explorations or action sequences based on themes from whatever they are studying. This of course is similar to making up games or holiday themes based on subject matter, but the idea of an adventure subtly shifts the focus toward a sequence of actions or experiences with an air of excitement, vigilance, risk, and so on. In addition, the idea of collaborating to make an adventure for other people as well as for oneself adds a very motivating and cooperative social dimension.

**NOTES**

**NOTES**

## The Play Plan

As one final example before turning to the source meta-plan that has been guiding us, try thinking of whatever you are doing as "playing" it. As we shall see, the Play AP has several versions; this one was suggested by a student several years ago. To illustrate this approach, think back to when you were a young child and excelled at pretending to be or do some "grown-up" thing or other. Thus you might have played at cooking, driving, teaching, or exploring the frontier. What if you now imagine that you are "playing" reading this book, teaching your actual classes, cleaning the house, writing letters, or whatever else comes your way? Might this offbeat way of thinking about what one is up to lead to a sense of fun in some unexpected places? Could we perhaps recapture some of the *joie de vivre* that came so readily during our play as children?

A related version of the Play Plan is to shift the meaning of play to a more adult form and think of whatever you are doing as a form of recreation or vacation activity. We tried this very successfully one year when the fall school term began in August, when summer still seemed in full swing. Rather than think of teaching as "going back to work," we viewed it as simply another phase of the vacation—rather like a visit to a participatory museum or amusement park where the exhibits or rides consisted of seeing what it was like to teach classes, attend committee meetings, and otherwise sample the academic life. Defining work as play in this way worked beautifully, and the summer was finished out in fine style; teaching, at least for a while, really did seem like a vacation activity.

A third, somewhat more "serious" version of the Play Plan is to regard your life as the unfolding of a dramatic play, so that you are an actor in an ongoing story (see also the Story Plan below). If nothing else, this is a great way to reduce anxiety in some difficult interpersonal situations. Simply imagine that you and the other participants are only actors in an improvisational scene. This can indeed help you stay calm in a variety of situations, including dealing with principals, parents, and even difficult students. And imagining that cameras are rolling while you're at it might add a touch of anxiety but can also help you keep your cool in emotional situations.

Academically enhancing all three versions of the Play AP is easily accomplished by calling up the cognitive strategy of "expert advice." To apply any subject area, ask yourself what sort of advice a specialist in that subject would give you. A mathematician, for instance, might suggest that you play more at proving your points as you teach; a historian might recommend playing at thinking of whatever you are doing as an event of historic proportions or perhaps imagining that a particular historic figure is tagging along on your vacation of the moment. What ideas for more fully utilizing the Play Plan might each of the following specialists offer you and your students?

## PHYSICIST

## ECONOMIST

## SPELLING EXPERT

## PHOTOGRAPHER

## HEALTH SPECIALIST

_____ **(other)**

[✎]

This AP can also help to bring academic content playfully to bear on life by temporarily thinking of your world as a _____ (academic subject area) playground. What happens when you (or your students) start to think of school or home as a math playground or a social studies playground or even a reading playground? What if you and your students viewed the world as a playground based on what you most (or least) love to teach?

[✎]

What new feelings and ideas for activities does the "playground" connotation evoke?

[✎]

### The Alternative-Meanings (Meta-)Plan

All four of the above related APs can be derived from the plan of deliberately thinking up alternative meanings. Each type of alternative meaning generates a new awareness plan. Thus, in dreaming up alternative meanings for situations or events, APs such as the following are readily created:

- **Regarding each day as a holiday**

- **Thinking of whatever is going on as a game (or as an adventure)**

- **Interpreting events as if they are part of a religious ritual**

- **Interpreting events as elements in psychology experiments (or as elements in practical jokes or "Candid Camera" setups)**

- **Viewing things as museum exhibits (see the next chapter)**

- **Thinking of whatever you are doing as a hobby**

- **Regarding life as an experiment (science), as history being made or as a political process (social studies), as solving simultaneous equations (math), and so on**

The Alternative Meanings Meta-Plan is indeed an extremely general AP generator. It can also serve as a guide for academic amplification of awareness plans. The key in this approach is to think of alternative themes or meanings for an awareness plan by drawing on academic subjects or content. Examples include academic themes for the Holiday, Game, Adventure, and Play plans discussed earlier.

We now turn to a different version of the Alternative Meanings Plan; this one is a meta-plan with a special flair.

### The Metaphor Meta-Plan

A metaphor, according to George Lakoff and Mark Johnson (1980), arises from experiencing and understanding something in terms of something else. Examples of common metaphors include thinking of argument as a kind of war ("shoot down your opponent's points," "defend your position"), regarding time as money ("wasting" or "spending" it, for example), and thinking of the mind as a box ("fill your mind with good ideas"). Creativity and playfulness can be cultivated (agricultural metaphor) by zapping (video game/cartoon metaphor) our thoughts with new metaphors. For instance, notice the new ideas and images that emerge when you try thinking of argument as dance, time as a fountain, and the mind as, let's say, a hunter.

Each new metaphor in fact elicits a new awareness plan or set of awareness plans. Calling the mind a hunter, for example, elicits its own conceptual framework for thinking about mental activity—presumably a much more active and aggressive way of thinking about the mind than is aroused by regarding it as a box. It is actually very easy to come up with new metaphors for anything. Since our minds (whatever they are!) are very good at forming connections, all we need to do is suggest a metaphorical pairing and connections will usually start popping up almost as if by magic (the mind as conjurer?). To demonstrate how this works, try using the items in column 2 in the list that follows as alternative metaphors for each item in column 1 and notice the varied interpretations thereby suggested:

| thought | (as) | joy ride |
|---------|------|----------|
| love | | equation |
| education | | carpet |
| politics | | symphony |
| death | | food |

Each of these interpretations represents the operation of a new awareness plan induced by the chosen metaphor. To think of politics as a carpet activates different conceptual connections—and hence a different AP—than does thinking of it as food or a joy ride.

Academic content can provide wide-ranging enhancement possibilities for this playful meta-AP. Simply draw on subject areas and content for new metaphors. If you wanted new ideas for how to view your day, for example, what metaphors might you draw from such areas as

**BIOLOGY?** (the day as a cell? or a developing organism?)

**GEOGRAPHY?** (the day as a country? a river?)

**PHYSICAL EDUCATION?** (the day as a sport? an exercise?)

```
✎
```

**LITERATURE?** (the day as a poem? a novel?)

```
✎
```

What are some inside-out activities or assignments that would help your students apply metaphors based on what you teach?

```
✎
```

We shall return to the Metaphor Meta-Plan in later chapters, but for now let's explore a very playful plan related to the literature metaphor.

**NOTES**

### The Story Plan

Human beings seem to thrive on stories. Much of our entertainment, religion, and conversation revolves around narrations and dramatizations of both true and imaginary sequences of events. Most of us are also very good at making things up ourselves, especially as children but throughout our lives to a considerable degree. In general, stories and story construction can contribute very positively to play and to playfulness in virtually all of its forms.

The Story AP, you may rightly guess, is to conjure up a story about _____ (whatever you select). Now, there are a great many ways to go about this process. One of our own favorites is to use what we call the "Book Title Plan." First, think of whatever you are focusing on as the title of a book. Thus while reading this book, you might come up with titles such as *The Page,* or *Reading,* or perhaps *The Strange Book.* Or if you were worried about a dentist's appointment, you might try titles like *Apprehension* or *The Gums Bite Back.* The title, however, is only the start. The important next step is to imagine your book under various literary genres, such as comedy, science fiction, romance, children's stories, and so on. For each genre, imagine what the book would be about. As science fiction, for instance, *The Strange Book* or *The Gums Bite Back* would likely suggest far different story lines than these same titles would as comedies or courtroom dramas. Starting with a title and genre gives a powerful boost to story-generating ingenuity and variety.

It is possible to enhance this AP academically in a couple of ways. One way is to use subject areas or specific content to suggest story elements or themes. For instance, social studies might lead you to think of various historical or political themes, while math might lead you to approach your story in a very logical, consistency-oriented fashion.

Perhaps an easier—and ultimately richer—approach to academic enhancement of the Story AP is to try taking on the role of an expert or key figure in a particular discipline as you compose your story. Ask yourself how that person would construct the story. Drawing on biology, say, you might try thinking of how Darwin would construct a story about apprehension or about reading (maybe focusing on how a particular emotion or skill "evolved" and "reproduced"). Or you might simply take on the general role and thought patterns of a biologist to direct your story toward the interaction of organisms, life processes, and the like.

Since this could be getting a little too serious for the playful theme of this chapter, let's turn to a more fanciful way to use roles to spice up one's experience of the world.

## Playful Role-Taking Plans

As discussed in chapter 2, one of the most powerful tools for creative thinking is to take on new mental roles as you generate new ideas or work on solving a problem. Mental role-taking can also be used for sheer fun and playfulness, though. Let's explore some ways.

For a simple warm-up, try looking at the world as if you were an animal—say, a parakeet, an ant, or a giraffe. What kinds of things would be important to you in each case?

What would your main fears and desires be?

What would you regard the behavior of human beings?

How would you regard the behavior of human beings?

What would strike you as humorous?

To carry this a step further, try taking on the mental role of your house or car, your clothing (shoes seem an especially interesting role, one group of teachers found), or your school building or playground. Again, in each role, what would be your fears, hopes, dreams, jokes, and view of people?

To go still farther afield (left field), how about taking on the mental role of anger, playfulness, love, inconsistency, or abstraction? What would you "hunt for" in each of these roles?

What would your worst fear and fondest wish be?

What would you do for fun?

How would you view yourself as you actually are?

Academic enhancement can be simply a matter of choosing items from various subject areas to suggest new roles. How about looking at life from the points of view of several authors or their fictional characters? Or what about viewing everyday situations and events as if you were gravity or oscillation or perhaps a cell nucleus or white corpuscle? Or a spelling error?

Our intent here is to treat the role-playing approach in a somewhat offbeat manner, but an obvious academic amplification is also to take on roles of various subject area specialists as a playful activity in itself. Just imagine yourself to be a mathematician, geographer, grammarian, or whatever, and go to it! For pedagogical purposes, even if you take the roles of academic concepts, it helps to take the role as if you were a specialist in the relevant field. How would a biologist view the world if she or he were a cell nucleus?

The purpose of all this "nonsense," again, is to take your mind on a little vacation to new locales, to jolt your usual categories of interpretation and judgment, and to have some fun. Such role-taking APs (each role generates its own set of specific awareness plans) can also serve educational purposes by offering lessons in taking alternative points of view, providing starting places for essays, and exploring new subject matter in a very lively manner.

Let's look at one more awareness plan—in this case a playfully practical one—and then explore some basic principles and an integrative lesson plan model.

## The New Uses Plan

The essence of this AP is to think up new uses for whatever you choose. This can actually lead to some seriously practical and inventive ideas, but for now let's just play. To begin, it helps a lot in thinking up new uses if you first narrow the intended purpose. Some examples of playful purposes for new uses would be new ways to use _____ as a toy, as an element in a practical joke, as part of a Halloween costume, as a component in a new game, or as a musical instrument or other art object or implement. How, for instance, might a clock (or even this book) be used in each of those ways?

The New Uses Plan is especially rich for playfully funneling academic content and roles into everyday life. In broad form, the academically amplified AP would be "think of new uses for _____ (whatever you choose) based on or related to

_____ (academic discipline or specific content)." What, for example, are some mathematical uses for this book (using the pages to count or measure?), or some biological uses (be careful how you answer that!), or some potential literary uses (building poems around some of the ideas?), or some uses based on specific concepts that you teach?

This approach can also provide an easy classroom demonstration of the power of academic content to boost creativity. As in our picture interpretation exercise in chapter 1, start by asking your students to list as many uses as they can for some common object, such as a desk or lamp. After they run dry, ask them to think of new uses a mathematician, biologist, historian, economist, and so on, might suggest. Or try asking your students to draw on a variety of roles based specifically on what you teach. Each new academic role will elicit still more new ideas for alternative uses.

It is productive and enjoyable to use this AP to help apply academics far and wide, as by looking for "subject uses" for people (how about new historical or mathematical uses for students?), activities (new economic or political uses for washing dishes or fixing cars?), emotions (new biological or musical uses for embarrassment?), and ideas (new poetic or foreign-language uses for scientific principles?). As the last example indicates, a possible academic use for the New Uses AP is to search out ways to use one subject area in the service of another—or to pose this to your students as a way to help them integrate and apply different areas of study.

With respect to the whole approach in this book, at a meta-level we can in fact think of our central endeavor as thinking up new creative-thought-enhancing uses for academic content and also new life- and education-enhancing uses for various awareness plans. And that (rather serious) idea brings us to a quick review of some basic principles, followed by a sample model for playful lesson plans.

## Basic Principles

We started this chapter with some principles of playfulness. Might we now go on to list some fundamentals of fun? Here are a few of our candidates:

- Fantasy and fun are close relatives. The importance of stories in art and entertainment helps to illustrate that. APs such as the Story Plan and the Adventure Plan, not to mention the Holiday and Play plans, are designed to help capture some usable fantasy and inject it into our daily living.

- The principles of playfulness apply to fun as well. Fun "works": it's a powerful way to enrich life. We must give ourselves and our students permission to have fun. Proactively choosing and creating it—as by developing and using playful APs—provide helpful assists. Practice definitely helps. And spreading and sharing fun wherever you can (proliferation) can work wonders for your own and others' lightheartedness.

- Getting too serious about fun can be self-defeating. The key, after all, is lightheartedness; cultivating a certain degree of nonchalance about life may be a good place to start (see also chapter 6).

- Mihaly Csikszentmihalyi's (1975, 1990) concept of "flow" can give us some important clues about fun. Flow includes a non-self-conscious absorption in an activity and seems

**NOTES**

**NOTES**

to arise in large part from a sense of exercising skill successfully in relation to a meaningful challenge. Hobbies, challenging work, and conversations with friends are some common sources. Deliberately using new awareness plans that positively influence the quality of your ongoing experience may also be a good flow generator. Playful APs and their academic enhancement may work especially well.

- Cooperation, because it—unlike competition—supports intrinsic motivation, should contribute to a social atmosphere conducive to fun. (See chapter 8 for further discussion.)

- Evidence concerning intrinsic motivation (for example, Amabile 1983; Deci and Ryan 1985) also points to the importance of voluntary choice in generating a sense of fun in any activity. It is hard to make people have fun, and it is harder to have fun in a forced activity than in a voluntary one.

## Sample Lesson Plan

Now let's see how all this might apply in teaching. Here is a sample model for lesson plans oriented toward infusing fun and playfulness into life with the help of academic subject matter:

**GOAL:** To inject more playfulness and fun into a specific aspect of life (say, arguing a personal point of view or enforcing rules on hall patrol), using academic subject areas as resources for enhancing playful ways of thinking

**SAMPLE PROCEDURE:** Divide the class into groups of three or four. Ask each group to think of things it would really like to have more fun at or approach more playfully and then to select one of these things for which to get further advice. Next ask each group to trade its selection with another group. Each group then works on advice about how the other group can reach its goal, basing this advice on academic amplifications of the types of APs discussed in this chapter. To add some flair to the whole procedure, have each group present a skit, such as a before-and-after TV commercial, that dramatizes a solution for the whole class.

**EXAMPLE:** Let's say you are teaching state history to a fifth-grade class. You could follow the above procedure and perhaps ask the groups to use the Game Plan or the Adventure Plan to help each other be more playful about their selected activities. Each group could then be instructed to tell how a key figure from your state's history might suggest making an adventure or a game out of the activity. In a high school English class, you could follow the same procedure, except that the suggestions for game or adventure themes would be drawn from the authors or literary characters under study. Other playful APs, such as the Holiday Plan or the Metaphor Plan, could of course also be used. Or students could be left more to their own devices and perhaps simply instructed to offer fun-enhancing advice based on the course's academic content.

**EVALUATION:** The students' skits and advice can be evaluated for the degree of understanding and use of subject content reflected in them. One of the best ways to do this is to ask the class to give each group feedback and suggestions concerning its use of the content. Another approach is to ask each student to write a short account of what he or she contributed to the group's advice and to add afterthoughts on how to use relevant academic content for further playfulness-enhancing ideas. As with any group activity, it also pays to get feedback and suggestions from the class concerning the value and possible improvement of the activity.

**FOLLOW-UP:** At the least, students can be asked to tell how they actually used any of the ideas generated by the groups. To go a bit further, students could make journal entries about any later applications or any related ideas pertaining to the activity. In addition, the students can be encouraged to try

**NOTES**

similar approaches with other subject matter and to invite friends or family members to join with them in using some of these playful ways of thinking.

What are some of your own ideas for inside-out ways to promote playfulness? If you were to make that a theme for some new lesson plans, whole units, casual questions or asides, or potential outreach suggestions, what might you do that could be fun and enlightening for both yourself and your students?

# Summary Awareness Plan Map

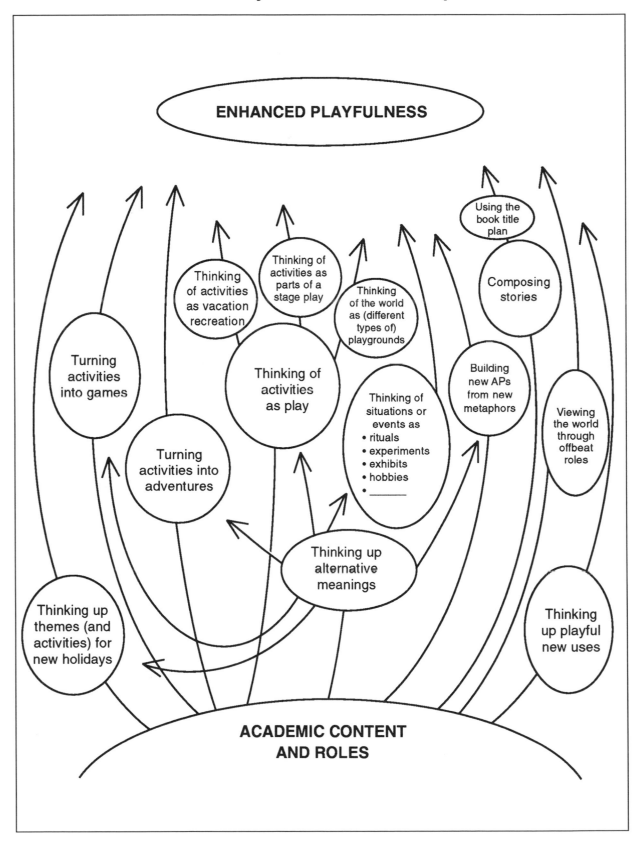

**ENHANCED PLAYFULNESS**

Using the book title plan

Composing stories

Thinking of activities as vacation recreation

Thinking of activities as parts of a stage play

Thinking of the world as (different types of) playgrounds

Turning activities into games

Thinking of activities as play

Thinking of situations or events as
• rituals
• experiments
• exhibits
• hobbies
• _____

Building new APs from new metaphors

Viewing the world through offbeat roles

Turning activities into adventures

Thinking up alternative meanings

Thinking up themes (and activities) for new holidays

Thinking up playful new uses

**ACADEMIC CONTENT AND ROLES**

# 4

# Learning for Interest and Appreciation

What are some awareness plans that enhance interest, insight, and appreciation? How can academic content enrich creativity in using these plans? What are examples of procedures and lesson plans that involve this process?

## Interest and Its Academic Enhancement

A. S. Neill (1960), founder of the famous alternative school Summerhill, has provocatively asserted that interest is the royal road to happiness. Why would this be so? Interest involves attention, awareness, curiosity, and active involvement. Moreover, it gives rise to emotions such as fascination and caring; it is a central contributor to appreciation. Interest is also at the heart of intrinsic motivation—enjoying an endeavor for itself rather than because of its consequences. And intrinsic motivation supports not only direct satisfaction in life but also creativity (see Amabile 1983, 1989), which in turn leads to solutions that can further enrich life. (See also Renninger, Hidi, and Krapp 1992 for a fine compendium of recent theory and research on interest and learning.)

Let us begin, then, with some very special awareness plans that bestow the power to enhance interest wherever they are used.

### Thinking Up Questions

**Try this:** Look around you right now and pick out some ordinary, not particularly interesting object. Without thinking about it too much, rate your level of interest in the object on a scale of 0 to 10, where 10 means being absolutely enthralled with interest and 0 corresponds to being bored stiff. Now start thinking up all the questions you can about the object. You don't need to come up with any answers; just think up questions one after another. (It is still in the spirit of this awareness plan to think of possible answers, but keep generating new questions as well.) Take about three or four minutes.

Welcome back! What rating on our 0 to 10 interest scale would you now give the object? Do you feel more curious about this object? Do you have a richer sense of what you know and don't know about it? Do you appreciate its interconnections with the world more than you did before this little exercise? These are some of the potential benefits from deliberately thinking up questions about something. Such benefits arise because question posing leads us to interconnect the object of the questions with things we already know and care about (assuming one is serious in using this AP).

A question you pose to yourself is also a lot like your own telephone ringing (well, before the days of answering machines). There's an urge to answer the darn thing. Attempting to answer a question activates a new awareness plan that is unique to each question.

Indeed, every question can easily be translated into an awareness plan. Some illustrations: Who made_____? = Remember or figure out who made _____. What's the best way to use _____? = Figure out alternative uses for _____ and pick out the best one. (Here's one for you to try: How do you turn any question into its corresponding awareness plan? = _____ .

```
✍
```

**A solution:** "Think up procedures for turning any question into its corresponding AP."

This tendency to answer posed questions carries a rather serious implication. Since trying to answer a question involves using an awareness plan determined by the question, and since an awareness plan is a way of using your mind at a given time, is not question posing a powerful way of guiding the use of one's own or other people's minds? (See what we mean?) Of course, if questions are used in the spirit of this AP—that is, to stimulate interest—lots of good can be done. We just mention this issue of "thought control" as a reminder that fiddling with awareness plans is serious business.

Now back to the enhancement of interest. What kinds of questions work best? (Notice this is a meta-question, a question about questions, although not necessarily about itself. How about: "What kinds of meta-questions work best?") Based on the rationale underlying the Question AP, one good starting place would be questions that link one's own areas of high interest to the object of the questioning (about which interest is to be increased). For example, if you or one

**NOTES**

of your students wanted to become more interested in the evening news, a good question to ask oneself might be "What links might each news story conceivably have with my favorite hobby or my favorite school subject?"

Another good starting place would be questions that challenge and stretch one's thinking or lead to provocative new perspectives. Examples might include "What are some unusual new uses for_____ (even newscasts!)?" or "What would so-and-so (fill in a favorite cartoonist, politician, character from literature or film, and so on) say or *ask* about _____?" This last question actually pushes us gently toward the next step: using academic content to enhance the Question Plan—and thus to increase interest in whatever you choose.

## Academic Enhancement of the Question AP

Obviously, if thinking up questions about everyday objects or situations can increase our interest in them, question posing about curricular content might increase interest in that, as well—especially if the interest seekers pose these questions for themselves. However, academic content can serve not just as the object of questions but perhaps much more powerfully as a resource for composing more interesting questions about *anything*.

To demonstrate what we have in mind, let's go back to the opening exercise for the Question Plan. Please take a moment to recall the "ordinary, not particularly interesting object" you selected and the questions you composed about it. (We do hope you did this. If not, please take a few minutes to try it now before reading further; it will make the next step more fun and more meaningful.)

Now, to enhance academically the Question AP you started with, try formulating questions that a physicist might ask or that are suggested to you by the field of physics, including its methods, areas of interest, specific key principles or concepts, or types of questions.

What are at least three such physics-inspired questions?

(Our own example for a desk lamp: How hot does it get? How could we measure the temperature? How does the temperature fluctuate with changes in line voltage?)

Now what further questions are suggested by social studies?

(A lamp example: How has electric lighting affected work habits?)

What queries might a geographer suggest?

Or think of a favorite work of literature. What questions about your object might the author or various characters in the work ask?

Obviously, any subject can suggest new questions. And the likelihood is that many of these questions will be genuinely new—questions that go beyond what you would think up off the top of your head. Therein lies the wondrous power academics can bestow on our use of this AP (and indeed on our use of just about any awareness plan).

How might you help your students use your subject matter to ask themselves interest-arousing questions about other subjects or about matters outside school?

Now let us take a look at a few other examples of awareness plans designed to enhance interest— and how to use academic subject matter to enhance these plans.

## *The Boring/Interesting Plan*

This time pick out the most boring things you can find around you right now, items that hover around the very bottom of the interest scale. Also think of the most boring aspects of the subjects you teach or your tasks as a teacher. See how long a list you can generate of low rollers in the interest sweepstakes.

What did you notice as you did this?

Many people, for instance, discover that actively searching for boring items is itself an interesting activity and that on even the slightest amount of further reflection many "candidates for boredom" seem a bit interesting after all. In fact, some people experience real difficulty in locating anything that seems genuinely boring. Nonetheless, virtually everyone can pinpoint some items and situations that are decidedly less interesting than others.

Next, select an item or two from your list that show promise of holding on to their low interest rating. The second part of our awareness plan, you may have guessed, is to look for hidden interesting aspects of these challenging items or to figure out some way to provoke interest in them. Note that simply searching for interesting aspects is a straight awareness plan, while thinking up ways to provoke interest—especially thinking up new ways to think that provoke interest—is in fact a meta-plan, a plan for generating other plans. As an example of this latter strategy, you might recall the Question Plan from the previous section and decide to use it to provoke your interest, or you might devise a new strategy such as imagining what young children would find interesting about your challenging items. Take a couple of minutes right now to see if you can raise your level of interest in the "boring" items you picked.

Did you succeed? Even a slight rise in interest counts, since it demonstrates your ability to influence consciously your interest level.

This particular AP is extremely easy to adapt for classroom use. Either in guided discussion or in a more organized gamelike activity, students can challenge each other to "go ahead and make my day; show me something interesting about _____ (an academic topic the challenger finds relatively boring)." Students can prove amazingly resourceful at provoking each other to find interesting qualities in subjects or interesting new ways to think about subjects. This activity can indeed serve as a mind-expanding arena for students to practice and share new APs, budding metacognitive skills, and even the academic enhancement process. And speak of the devil:

## Academic Enhancement of the Boring/Interesting AP

It is one thing to increase interest about school subjects; it is a much broader challenge to use school subjects to help increase interest about other matters, even extending to life outside school. The essential process for academically enhancing the Boring/Interesting Plan is to employ the meta-plan of using academic content to suggest interesting ways to think about whatever you find boring.

Let's say you or your students think waiting in line is boring and would like it to seem more interesting. Here are some ways academics might help in using the Boring/Interesting AP:

- Drawing on the domain of physics, look around for all the ways in which gravity is affecting objects or people around you. Or more generally, look for all the types of energy transfer you can find. Or conjure up images based on "physics-fiction" questions, such as "What if acceleration of falling objects *decreased* after an initial burst of speed?" or "What if you could see sounds and hear colors?" (Notice this last example is also a special use of the Question AP.)

- Now pulling from the world of young children's literature, you might try thinking of what fairy tale or fairy-tale character each person around you would best fit or be. Or you could use the waiting situation itself to inspire an idea for a story modeled after one of your favorite children's stories or any story recently read in school.

- Gathering suggestions from the role of historian, perhaps try figuring out probable pasts for each of the people or objects around you. Or imagine how each person or thing would fit in or affect different historical situations. Or just think of how people from various historical periods might react if suddenly transported to your waiting situation. Can you look at the surroundings as they might? What would they find especially interesting, based on what you know of their historical context?

As we pointed out, the underlying meta-plan in these examples is to use academic content to think up potentially interesting ways to think about waiting situations. However, several specific guiding APs are also embedded in the above examples. You might enjoy picking some of these out before reading further.

Here is a list of some of these guiding awareness plans used in the above examples to help carry out the master plan of finding interest in a boring situation. Each plan is also "academically enhanced":

- Use concepts from _____ (academic discipline) to notice things you normally wouldn't.

- Think up "what if" questions based on reversals or interchanging of principles or phenomena from _____ (academic discipline).

- Think up parallels or appropriate contexts from _____ (academic subject) for people or things in the situation you are trying to make more interesting.

- Make up a story suggested by the situation, using concepts or forms from _____ (academic domain) to shape the story.

- Challenge yourself to figure out something about the situation, using the basic questions of_____ (academic discipline) as a guide.

- Think of how the people or things studied in _____ (academic field) would perceive or react to the situation if they could; mentally take on their roles and use those roles to find new interesting aspects of the situation.

The above plans are presented in the sequence they appear in the previous examples from physics, children's literature, and history, but these underlying academically enhanced APs are now presented in a more general format so that each one can be used with any academic field as the enhancer. Each could also be the basis for an in-class activity or a homework assignment.

## Aesthetic Appreciation and Its Academic Enhancement

In addition to interest, appreciation also includes an aesthetic component—a savoring of the qualities, patterns, meanings, and interconnections of whatever we attend to. There are many theories about what underlies aesthetic experience. Some theorists give greatest weight to the sheer delight of sensory qualities and forms, without reference to the functions or other normal meanings we attach to things (see, for example, Osborne 1970; Franck 1973). Other theorists stress the role of meaning in artistic expression and experience; aesthetic satisfaction for them arises from an expansion in one's sense of understanding and insight (see, for instance, Kreitler and Kreitler 1972). All considered, both meaning and form seem involved in aesthetic awareness—taking joy in both the physical characteristics and the associations we experience.

There can be little doubt that aesthetic experience, whatever its ultimate nature, contributes greatly to the quality of life. Nonetheless, in school and elsewhere in our society, aesthetics often seems compartmentalized and tied mostly to visual arts and music. It is quite possible, however, for aesthetically toned thought, perception, and action to infuse anything we wish. For instance, as the following "Reflections" exercise demonstrates, you can view problems as art forms, academic subjects as containing both art forms and whole new art modes, and even education itself as art.

**NOTES**

**Reflections on Art Forms and Academics:** What's special about art forms?

Some of our thoughts: Art forms tend to evoke active, thoughtful perception for both the beholder and the creator. There's an inherent beauty or valued meaning associated with art forms. When art forms are created by skilled artists, beholders often feel inspired; even children's art can inspire a sense of appreciation and awe. Art forms communicate (often ineffable ideas and feelings) and seem to connect us as humans; they may even be unique to humans. Art forms are multifaceted (as humans are) and seem to invite extended contemplation. They also touch something universal; every culture creates art forms. Moreover, the person who creates or appreciates art forms gets "richer" with increased exposure and understanding.

What are your thoughts?

It is possible to find—or to make up—an art form unique to practically anything, including academic subjects. Here is an activity to illustrate what we have in mind and how it might be useful:

*Step 1:* Take a couple of minutes to write about something that consumes you, some aspect of your life that is problematic for you, for which you want advice or strategies on how to handle it better.

*Step 2:* Now think of how that problem might be an art form. Jot down ideas about the skills involved in creating or appreciating the problem, the intricate (or simple) form of the problem, subtle interesting (perhaps even beautiful) aspects of the problem, possible sources of awe the problem provides, and so on.

*Step 3:* Now think about academic subjects as art forms, or what possible art forms or whole new art modes might be associated with specific disciplines. Write down your ideas about art forms or modes that are unique to a given academic discipline or subject area. For example: geography—cartography or customs as art; math—constructing proofs or graphs as an art mode, formulae as art forms; biology—genetic engineering or ecological relations as art; psychology—awareness planning as a new art mode, or emotions, motives, and dreams as art forms.

*Step 4:* Now apply what you have discovered in step 3 to the problem you noted in step 1 and step 2. Take a few minutes to write or draw your reflections about how some of the academic art forms or modes from step 3 might express or portray your problem. For example, cartography might suggest drawing some sort of map of your problem or how it arose; math might suggest symbolizing your issue in a formula of some kind. Also note any new solution ideas such representations suggest.

*Step 5:* Take a moment to evaluate your experience. Did you gain any new ideas—or new appreciation—for your problem? Do you feel more interested in the academic subjects you noted? Do you want to know more about their "art forms"? Can you see a kind of meta-art in the very process of finding or creating such new art modes? How might you make further use of this approach in your classroom and your life?

What are some adaptations of this exercise that could be used as activities or assignments for your students?

The underlying awareness plan here, of course, is to think of everything as art or as a source of artistic inspiration. With just a slight twist, this AP yields our next special awareness plan (and path for using academics to increase appreciation).

## *The Museum Exhibit Plan*

Look around right now and imagine that any object or even the whole scene is actually an exhibit in an art museum. Then ask yourself why this object or scene might have been selected as worthy of museum purchase and display. (Important: Just assume that it is worthy; your job is to figure out why it is.) For instance, the little paperback *Webster Handy College Dictionary* sitting on top of the upside-down *Roget's College Thesaurus* could have been chosen for its spectacular combination of blue, yellow, and red rectangles in a three-dimensional array; or perhaps it symbolizes the dominance of "correct" single-mindedness (dictionary definitions) over more free-form thought patterns (represented by the "underling" thesaurus). Now, what rationales are there for *your* museum exhibit?

This AP to view _____ (whatever you choose) as an exhibit in an art museum derives its power from the way art museums can frame or define virtually anything as art and from the ability all of us have to reframe mentally at will. Notice you can also redefine objects very easily not only as art but also as, say, weapons or as game equipment or toys. Once you have allowed for the even imaginary possibility that _____ could be considered a weapon or a work of art, it is usually a simple matter to conjure up a rationale to justify that interpretation. Again, as Edward de Bono and other creativity theorists have noted (see chapter 2), our minds are terrific at forming connections once we have picked the points to connect. And that observation brings us to the use of academic content to enhance the Museum Plan.

**NOTES**

## Academic Enhancement of the Museum AP

First, it should be clear that the Museum AP is readily applicable to academic content as a possible focus for aesthetic contemplation. Books and topics of study can be viewed as art exhibits; concepts and principles can be written out or illustrated and made into artistic collages, songs, or other exhibits; and so on. However, to turn the content of education outward to enrich life, a somewhat different strategy is helpful.

This strategy is to view _____ (whatever you or your students would like to appreciate more) as an exhibit not necessarily in an art museum but rather in a museum devoted to a particular academic subject area. Thus, on a long hike or car trip, you might regard the passing scenery as containing various exhibits in a history, science, or geography museum, relating scholastic content to help flesh out the rationale—and thus your appreciation—for why each exhibit is a good choice.

Let's explore a little further how this works in practice. First, locate or think of something you would like to experience with more intellectual depth and richness—perhaps a situation or task you normally find dull or trying. Then imagine finding this situation in various museums defined by academic subjects, such as a math museum, a science museum, or even a literature museum. What special qualities or connections does each type of museum highlight? How does each museum offer the potential for greater appreciation of your chosen exhibit?

For an example, let's say you pick "correcting" (giving feedback on) students' work. You can apply the Museum Plan in at least two different ways. One way is to think of the work itself as the exhibit, an orientation that might not only make the work seem more interesting but also suggest some unusual comments for the students. A second approach is to view your own process of giving feedback as the exhibit, in which case you may start to regard the task as more intriguing than usual.

Here's how the first approach might work. Imagine you're reading students' reports about a field trip of some sort. What happens if you think of these reports as exhibits in, say, a science museum? You might then pose questions such as the following to yourself (each question of course carrying its own awareness plan): "What scientific concepts and principles do the reports illustrate?" (Perhaps the contents will include reference to biological or chemical phenomena, or the form of the report will remind you metaphorically of crystalline structures or the interaction between insects and flowers.) "What is unique or special about each report (or the whole group of reports) that would warrant its inclusion in a science museum?" "If these reports were somehow part of a scientific experiment or demonstration being displayed in the museum, what might that exhibit be and why?"

Or if you were to imagine the reports as exhibits in a geography museum, you might conjure up questions such as these: "What is special about the locations mentioned or implied in each report?" "What might each report reveal about the home environment or cultural background of its author?" "What might the group of reports illustrate about the region the authors now live in?" "What captions of geographical tone might go with each report?"

Now what questions would you offer for

**a math museum**

**a music museum**

**a literature museum**

**or an "academic errors" museum?**

NOTES

What other museum types would be appealing to apply, and what sorts of questions (implied awareness plans) would accompany each type?

Let's now look at the second approach: thinking of your own activity of giving feedback as the museum exhibit. In this case, you will regard your own thought and behavior as the display. What if you saw your paper correcting as an exhibit in a literature museum? (Perhaps your every comment and notation to the student could somehow be regarded as poetry, or you might view your activity as part of the process for shaping great writers of the future.) Or how about a physiology exhibit, in which case your activities might be illustrating all sorts of small muscle motions in the hands (and face?), not to mention various types of brain activity? Or you might try viewing your feedback giving as a psychology museum exhibit, perhaps then noting how well your behavior, thought, and feelings illustrate all sorts of mental and social processes. (Indeed, we can see some of the exhibit captions now: "Surprise at Student's Choice of Words," "Utter Frustration," "Joy at Seeing Something Click," "One More Attempt to Clarify.")

What new museum types and exhibit questions come to mind for you now? Do take a few minutes to reflect and maybe try out a couple of your own ideas on how to use academically enhanced versions of the Museum AP.

And now for something more. Here is a sample lesson plan for sharing this AP with students:

## Sample Lesson Plan Using the Museum AP

**GOAL:** To increase self-insight and self-esteem, using academic content and the Museum AP as tools

**PROCEDURE:** Working in pairs, students help each other figure out why various successes each has experienced would make interesting and appropriate exhibits in a museum of _____ (fill in with current academic content you are teaching). Each student then writes a review of the museum exhibits or, for early grade levels, draws a picture and caption representing each exhibit.

**NOTES**

**EXAMPLES:**
High school chemistry class—students review success in getting a job or a date as a metaphorical exhibit of molecular formation, complete with detailed use of chemical concepts (such as ionic or covalent bonding) that might parallel the social processes.

Primary grade spelling lesson—students find personal successes (such as meeting a deadline) that involve or otherwise illustrate spelling words ("deadline"?) they have yet to learn; the words throw new light on their successes, and the success exhibits suggest vivid images to help them remember the words.

**EVALUATION:** Ask students to rate the degree to which the exercise affected the salience of their past successes, their self-confidence, their feelings about themselves and their partners, and their understanding and interest regarding the academic subject matter. Also ask them to report and reflect on how their understanding of the subject contributed to any new insights about themselves or their successes: does more knowledge about the academic subject provoke more self-insight and enjoyment in doing the exercise? Also check with them about other types of applications they can generate for the Museum AP used in this exercise and about how other academic subjects might contribute.

Ask yourself how interesting and informative students' products are—what they tell you about the students as people and about their understanding of the subject matter.

**FOLLOW-UP:** Think of variations on the goal or process of this exercise. What are other aspects of students' lives that could benefit by being regarded as exhibits in a subject-area museum? What are various types of products or even projects that could arise from this type of exercise? How else might students work together in formulating and communicating their exhibit ideas? What types of in-class or homework activities might support generalization of subject matter to other subject areas and to real-life application? How might your students help in suggesting follow-up ideas? What other questions can you think of now that would help you devise further follow-up ideas?

## More Aesthetic APs and Their Academic Enhancement

Here are a few additional awareness plans that can help funnel academic content to enhance the appreciation of everyday things and situations. In each case try plugging in some of your favorite curricular content to amplify the plan, and then actually use the enhanced plan for a few minutes to see how it works in practice.

- **Figuring out unique or special qualities for _____ (whatever you would like to appreciate more).** This AP is an excellent way to open your senses and thoughts to the functional and intrinsic values of anything you pick. For instance, a common doormat can be a thing of nearly exquisite beauty if you stop to consider how it helps you keep the interior of your house clean. To enhance this awareness plan academically, simply use a subject area to help define the special qualities you search out. The enhanced plan would thus read "figuring out unique or special _____ (mathematical, historical, geographical, and so forth) qualities for _____ (whatever you choose)." A doormat, for example, then might be seen as having special historical properties (the notable people who "scraped here") in addition to its basic function. What special _____ (fill in a favorite academic subject area) qualities can you now think of for, say, a troublesome daily task or a difficult person you know?

- **Finding inspiration for an aesthetic creation from _____ (whatever you would like to appreciate more).** If you try thinking of yourself as any type of artist (sculptor, poet, movie maker, fashion designer, you name it), you might be amazed at how easy it is to derive ideas for creations in that art mode from just about anything you attend to. As a fashion designer, for instance, a lamp might suggest iridescent highlights for clothing, or a cutting remark might lead you to envision a new sophisticated tattered style. Anything can be grist for creative aesthetic thinking—and thereby gain some aesthetic value itself. To embellish this plan with academic content, base your "art" on whatever subject area you choose. An example would be "finding inspiration for a geographical creation from _____." The nasty remark might then be used to suggest, say, a vacation based on "nasty" weather locales (taking the geographical "artist" role of a vacation designer). What

artist modes do other academic disciplines—
such as chemistry, biology, or physical
education—suggest?

How might each new academic artist role help you
derive inspiration, and hence greater appreciation,
from _____ (maybe your most pressing current worry
or your most dreaded task)?

**Note:** An excellent in-class activity based on the
above AP is to organize the class in groups of three
students who imagine themselves to be great artists of
whatever type they choose or are assigned, each artist
type to be based on some aspect of the class's subject
areas. Each group selects something in everyday life

all three members would genuinely like to appreciate more and then passes that item to another group as a challenge ("commission") to work on. Each group then works together, always building on each member's ideas (since each is a great artist of her or his type) to generate a vision of a magnificent public work of art that celebrates the commissioned item and that embodies the art forms of each group member. Groups then share their final artistic visions, inspiring new appreciation for the things each group originally wanted to appreciate more.

To use this exercise as an inside-out educational tool, ask your students to choose artist roles based on whatever they are studying. In elementary classrooms, they might take on such roles as a "preposition artist," creating artworks that involve all sorts of prepositions, or an "arithmetic artist," who uses numbers or perhaps addition and subtraction to make art. For high school students, sample roles might be "physics artists," who create art based on the subject matter of physics textbooks and labs, or "world-history artists," creating art suggested by historical events or people. Student groups can then use these roles to generate visions of imaginary museums, parades, films, theme parks, music videos, or whatever, that celebrate things they would like to appreciate more—rainy weather, political campaigns, younger siblings, homework, or anything else they choose. What results might this activity have for your students' attitudes toward subject matter as well as toward the things in life they would like to appreciate more?

- **Thinking of what values would lead you to find beauty in _____ (whatever you would like to appreciate more).** For instance, a sadistic satirist might find genuine beauty in a biting remark. Or a person from a pre-industrial culture might find great wonder and beauty in modern plumbing or electrical fixtures. To enhance this AP academically—to use it as a channel for applying subject matter—how would you rephrase the plan?

Please think of your answer to the preceding question before reading the following academic amplification: "thinking of values based on _____ (academic subject area) that would lead to finding beauty in _____ (item to be appreciated more)." An example could be finding beauty in a dull task based on mathematical "values" of symmetry, repetition, or null sets (no joy in the task!), or perhaps based on geological "values" of slow erosion (of patience) or build-up of pressure (irritation). The essence of this approach is to envision a value system based on key concepts from the subject area that are somehow consistent with the item you wish to appreciate more. This can lead to at least a momentary shift to more positive feelings toward the item; this shift can serve as a kind of emotional circuit breaker, demonstrating experientially that more appreciative orientations are possible.

## Underlying Principles

What are the psychological and pedagogical principles that have guided this chapter's selection of awareness plans, academic enhancements, and sample educational suggestions?

Central to our approach is the psychological principle that **metacognition in the service of intrinsic motivation enriches life and creativity**. In other words, deliberately choosing awareness plans designed to boost interest and enjoyment can improve both the quality of your ongoing experience and the creativity of your thinking. This principle is based on a combination of our research and theory on metacognition and quality of life (see Leff 1978, 1984, 1986; Nevin and Leff 1990; Teresa Amabile's 1983, 1989 extensive work on intrinsic motivation and creativity). The specific awareness plans discussed in this chapter were chosen to exemplify mental strategies designed to enrich interest and enjoyment.

Another major psychological principle—and the one that underlies academic enhancement of APs—is that **building on new conceptual networks enhances creative thinking**. As many creativity theorists have argued (see chapter 2), our minds are very good at making connections, provided we give ourselves things to connect. By deliberately connecting academic content—a domain exceptionally rich in new and complex concepts—with awareness plans designed to enhance ongoing experience, we increase the usefulness and creative power of both the academic content and the awareness plans. We thereby also enrich our lives and increase our intrinsic motivation to learn and employ more academic content (along with more metacognitively chosen awareness plans). The result thus also includes greater self-empowerment and intellectual growth.

One of our primary pedagogical principles is that **cooperative learning and thinking facilitate these processes of metacognitive development, self-empowerment (and other-empowerment), and intellectual growth**. Evidence for this idea has been building for many years. (See chapter 8 for further discussion of this principle.) Most of our sample lesson plans include some aspect of cooperative learning.

A second major pedagogical guideline for us is to **involve students in active experimentation and use of subject matter and new awareness plans**. The notion of "learn by doing" is of course at the heart of this approach. As elaborated in chapter 8, we also encourage the use of multiple, varied modes of expression—journals, artwork of all kinds, various discussion formats, and so on.

We conclude with another sample lesson plan to illustrate these principles once more.

## Illustrative Lesson Plan

**GOAL:** To use academic disciplines to increase appreciation for something considered unavoidable but bothersome—for example, onerous rules

**SAMPLE PROCEDURE** (written here as instructions to students, using multiple disciplines): Working independently, free-write for five minutes about how rules affect your life, noting especially the rules that you find most difficult to follow.

Working with a partner, compare your lists of "onerous rules." Rate the rules according to how much (or how little) you appreciate these rules. Apply an appreciation rating scale, using 0 for totally boring to 10 for enthralling.

Working with your partner, list all the academic subjects you know that use rules (for example, spelling rules, rules of English grammar, the rules of syntax in any foreign language, arithmetic rules, algebra rules, the rules of historically tracing an event, science rules). Think of other kinds of rules also (for instance, rules of sports such as baseball and basketball, home rules, classroom rules, food rules, and so on).

Now work with your partner to think of how a variety of specialists might look at some of these rules. What would each type of specialist find

**NOTES**

**NOTES**

interesting or valuable about each set of rules? What kinds of questions might each type of specialist ask? For instance, a math specialist might symbolize the rules of English as equations and ask questions about how consistent the rules are. A geographer or historian might wonder where and how the rules originated. Take about five minutes to brainstorm as many types of questions and interesting observations as you can about rules, using these specialist roles as your guide.

Now work with your partner to figure out what kinds of exhibits various academic experts might create for these rules. For instance, consider how a French expert would arrange exhibits in a Museum of English Rules in contrast to how a geologist might arrange exhibits. Or how would an English literary expert exhibit rules of scientific method? (Perhaps by writing a short story or a fable for each rule?— A Museum of Fables of Scientific Methods.) A chemist might think of a rule laboratory to discover how to break down rules into their component parts. Or a biologist might turn the rules into a zoo, putting them in cages appropriate to their character. What rules slither like a snake or charge like an elephant? A musician might create a Symphony of Rules—what kind of tune would you put your rules to? Take about ten minutes to come up with as many different types of rule exhibits as you can, using as many different specialist roles as you and your partner can think up. Try drawing some quick sketches of your exhibit ideas.

Working independently again, rate your current appreciation of your list of Onerous Rules and free-write about how your thinking has changed toward the rules and academic subject matter you used. Also consider what other things in your life "academic expert" questions and exhibit ideas might help you appreciate more.

**EVALUATION:** Read samples of the students' free-writing (and any follow-up journals) to gain insight into their range of rules, academic subject applications, and results.

**FOLLOW-UP:** A week or so later, you might repeat this lesson to note any changes in what is listed as an onerous rule, what academic subject matter is applied, and so on. You can also check to see if appreciation for rules has changed, whether interest in the subject matter has increased, and if students are using academic roles to enrich their thinking and interest outside school. To expand the procedure, try focusing the activity on a new topic, such as boring tasks, daily hassles, or social problems. Perhaps also explore with your students how they might use what they've learned to help people outside the class develop the ability to generate appreciation and interest.

Does this lesson plan actually embody the underlying principles listed in the prior section?

How would you improve or adapt this plan for use in your own teaching (perhaps, say, using a single subject area as the source of specialist roles)?

What other teaching ideas—based on the themes and awareness plans in this chapter—come to mind for helping students use academic content to enrich their interest and appreciation in any area of life they choose?

# Summary Awareness Plan Map

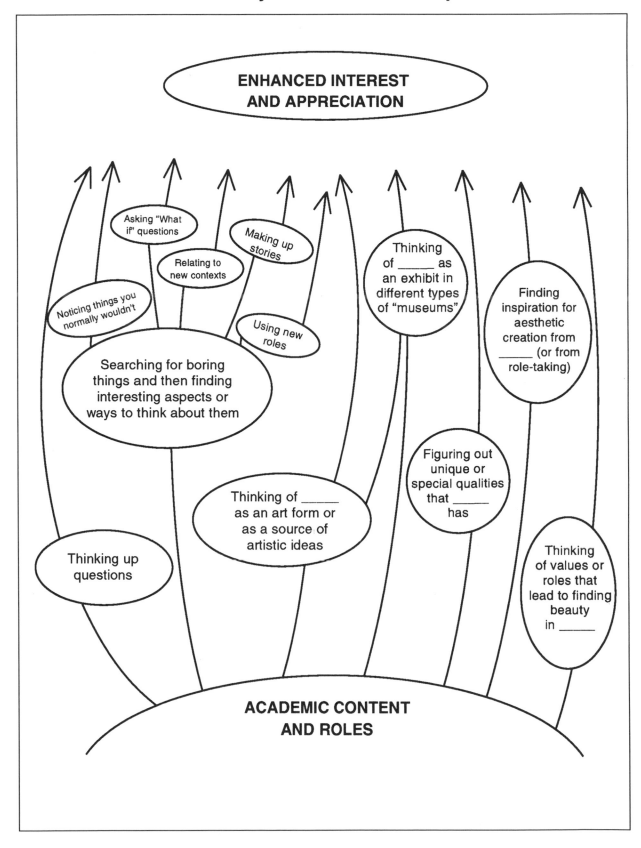

# 5

# Learning for Open-Mindedness

How can academic subject matter be used to expand open-mindedness, to increase empathy and understanding concerning others' values and points of view, and to expand judgmental flexibility? What are some awareness plans and lesson plans that can facilitate this type of academic application?

## Open-Mindedness

In the spirit of open-mindedness, we would say that it is wise to explore even the possibility that it is not so wise to be open-minded. Open-mindedness means receptivity to new or alternative ideas—and that, it seems to us, entails never being absolutely sure (although we sometimes have our doubts about this!).

Our favorite metaphor for open-mindedness is actually keeping open a "window of uncertainty"— uncertainty about your own beliefs and assumptions and uncertainty that people with whom you disagree are wrong. To be functional, though, this window does not have to be wide open; even a sliver of an opening can let in fresh ideas. The value of such willingness to entertain alternative possibilities is as follows:

**NOTES**

1. **It contributes to creativity** (as creativity specialists like Roger von Oech and Edward de Bono have pointed out, a crucial block to generating new solutions or ideas is thinking you already have the one and only answer);

2. **It contributes to communication and cooperation,** since others' ideas will be seen as worth considering;

3. **It contributes to learning,** since new information and ideas will be seen as possibly having real value;

4. **It contributes to richer experiences,** since you will be open to trying out new perspectives.

In addition to consideration of alternative ideas and perspectives, open-mindedness includes flexibility in forming judgments and evaluations. Open-minded individuals will be willing and able to assess people, ideas, and situations from a variety of angles. Again, this sort of mental agility contributes both to creativity and to constructive communication and empathy.

## Using Academic Subjects to Help Open One's Mind

If open-mindedness is indeed worth pursuing, how exactly can academic content and roles help out? Let's start with ways to add flexibility to evaluations and value judgments and then proceed to opening the window of uncertainty.

### Forming New Categories and Scales for Evaluating

How might various academic specialties evaluate love? Some possibilities: *Geology*—a Richter-scale rating scheme for the emotional intensity of a relationship; mineral or landform metaphors to characterize relationships (for example, "shale" versus "granite" or "volcano" compared with "eroding mountain"). *Biology*—a red corpuscle count for the viability of a relationship; animal metaphors for the nature of the relationship (compare an elephant of a love affair with a butterfly romance or a dandelion tryst). *History*— the "lastingness" of a relationship; characterization by different types of origination of the relationship; degree of documentation over time of feelings within the relationship; metaphorical characterization in terms of historical figures, events, or ideas (a Napoleonic or Manifest Destiny pattern for romance, for instance). What suggestions from your favorite (or most "volcanic") subject can you offer?

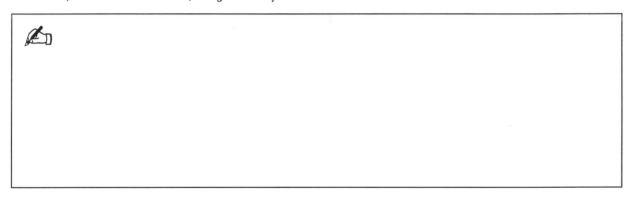

The underlying awareness plan here is to **think up unusual, academically based categories, rating scales, and metaphors for characterizing and evaluating anything you pick**. The underlying purpose of doing this is to increase one's openness, flexibility, and creativity in making judgments. So often in our culture we tend to evaluate in black-and-white categories such as "good" versus "bad," "right" versus "wrong," and "true" versus "false." By dipping into academic domains for some new, even outlandish, ideas for ways to make judgments, we can seriously open our minds.

Indeed, expanding judgmental complexity and discrimination can be useful even for such purposes as reducing prejudice. As Ellen Langer (1989) has so insightfully argued, prejudice often rests on making simplified, global judgments; if people use many different types of categories in evaluating other people, they are less likely to form stereotyped, prejudicial conclusions. We would add that using conceptually rich and unusual new categories, such as those so easily derived from academic subjects, can help both broaden and lighten up the whole process of forming judgments. Once again, academic content can put us in contact with the rich variety and possibilities inherent in the world.

Let's conclude with some of your examples. What new types of categories and scales for evaluating and characterizing your students' work can you derive from

**geometry?**

**geography?**

**social science?**

**literature (your favorite genre)?**

**your least favorite (or volcanic) subject?**

**_____?**

## Trying on Different Values

Probably most of us humans tend to assume that what we think is right or valuable really *is* right or valuable. It is often hard to step back from our ongoing sentiments to recognize the subjective character of value judgments. Actually, there is clearly room for debate about whether moral judgments are innately subjective, but our focus here is more on judgments of what is important or valuable than on those involving ethical determinations. With just a little meta-awareness it is fairly easy to recognize what each of us contributes to our sense of what is important. All you need to do is reflect on how what is important to you has changed over the years.

Curricular content can readily be applied to help broaden one's sense of what *might* be important—and in the process give some helpful practice in both open-mindedness and in expanding awareness in general. Indeed, this application represents one of the most direct uses of academic role perspectives that we can offer. Here are some examples of how it can work:

What if the subject matter of _____ were the most important thing in life? How would you regard the world? What would you notice? How would you make judgments? What would matter to you? For instance, if the subject of Roman history dominated your life and values, what would your values be? Some possibilities: You might cherish anything related to Latin, to Italy, to empire building, to gladiatorial combat (boxing and wrestling?), to dissolute lifestyles, or to the themes of early Christianity. In contrast, if the field of ecology dominated your value system, you might judge everything by its contribution to pollution or resource consumption, and you might be especially alert to the interactions of any organism with its environment.

An intriguing variation of this use of subject areas is to imagine what the whole society would be like if it were devoted to the subject content of a particular field. Imagine a society based on total absorption with mathematics, for instance. Would the TV sitcoms, soap operas, news, and talk shows center around the latest proofs or problems in topology? Would we speak and write in number codes? Would our religions employ mathematical symbols and processes as holy ceremonial elements? Or what if our society's value system were based on chemistry, or on music, or on French literature? Each subject area can suggest some wild and provocative possibilities that can increase both our awareness of alternatives and our appreciation for what our culture does now value. How might you build on this idea with your own students?

## Throwing New Light on Old Values

In addition to suggesting whole new value perspectives, subject areas and content can be used to look at both personal and cultural values from fresh points of view. What, for instance, are "historical" aspects of your current values (say, the role memory or the past serves in your values, or what might be even vaguely "Napoleonic"—or "Roman"— about your current values or those of the society)? How "biologically" oriented are your own values or those of the society at large? And what issues might a strongly biological perspective raise about these sets of values? Biology might, for example, suggest looking at the role health concerns play in your value system or how important the well-being of animals or ecosystems is.

Gaining deep insight into personal and societal values is quite challenging in many cases. Values, it turns out (see Leff 1978, chapter 4, for a review), come in both espoused and operative form. Espoused values are what people say is valuable, while operative values are what their actual behavior implies they find valuable. For real values clarification it helps to gain insight into both types of values and to notice any disparities. Such awareness can contribute to open-mindedness by helping individuals observe (and perhaps question) the operation of their own value systems from a distance.

Using roles and ideas from various academic areas can be a powerful tool for gaining this distance and for suggesting new places to probe. Even the methods from various disciplines might prove useful in analyzing social and personal values. Math, for instance, might suggest using graphs to plot the relations between espoused and operative values, and various sciences might lead to performing experiments to check on how important something really is to oneself or to other people. The interest and question components of academic roles can also be very useful. What might Dickens or Dickinson notice or ask about your values or those of our society?

What metaphors might a meteorologist or oceanographer offer for your values?

What value insights could your students gain from taking perspectives based on the subject matter you teach?

### Opening the "Window of Uncertainty"

The most direct way to use academic subjects and roles to increase open-mindedness may sometimes, rather paradoxically, violate a key principle of creativity enhancement. That principle, discussed further in chapters 2 and 7, is to build on ideas and to focus first on what is right with an idea. When applied to other people's ideas, this principle does support open-mindedness. But to increase uncertainty about one's own pet ideas—and hence to bolster open-mindedness—it can sometimes be useful to reverse this positive reception and be downright critical of what you yourself believe. Since such self-critiquing can be a real challenge, academic roles and content may prove to be helpful resources.

The guiding awareness plan for this rather perverse use of subject matter can be stated as follows: **Figure out ways to raise doubts about one's own beliefs from the perspective of _____ (academic discipline).** We must acknowledge that this plan really is perverse and should certainly be used with caution. You should keep firmly in mind that its purpose is not to undermine your beliefs and values but to create a mind-opening healthy skepticism— just enough so that you can be a little more open and curious concerning what other people have to say. It is only absolute certainty that is a threat to being open-minded. There is no need to stultify oneself; a little wedge of doubt is all that is needed!

Okay, so how can someone use academic areas as such a mind-opener via this perverse AP? Let us count some ways:

1. Cognitive developmental psychologists such as Mary Belenky and her colleagues (1986) have pointed out that as people become more mature and sophisticated in how they view knowledge, they tend toward the realization that "truth" is a human construct. Along the way, however, most of us will pass through various stages, usually including the orientation that knowledge is a fairly cut-and-dried matter of learning from authorities "in the know." Certainly our cultural tradition of a bucket-filling model of education (students as empty vessels into which teachers and texts pour truth) contributes to this epistemological viewpoint.

   However, if students explore the actual processes of theory, research, and interpretation in any academic field—and compare those with their own thought processes—they can form a more open view of how knowledge is created. They can learn to see the role of mental constructs, varying interpretation, and continuing historical change in what is regarded as "the truth." Such a realization of the way truth evolves and depends on human agreement can in itself be a tremendous mind

**NOTES**

opener, since it paves the way for questioning any assumption or belief and for exploring for truth cooperatively with other people. Any part of the curriculum can support this process by using academic content to reveal the constructed nature of human knowledge.

2. Once students realize the role of subjectivity, agreement, and interpretation in academic subject areas, they can be encouraged to use the AP of **critiquing their own beliefs as various types of academic specialists would**. For instance, the historian might suggest searching for ways to check the correctness of memories used to support attributions about other people, or looking for possible alternative explanations for past occurrences. Taking the role of an astronomer might similarly lead to the idea that one's beliefs may be a little like light from a distant star: some beliefs may actually radiate from the past and no longer accurately portray the way things are. Roles from experimental sciences might of course suggest forming and testing hypotheses based on one's beliefs to see if they really hold up. Even generating ideas for such experiments might help introduce healthy skepticism concerning beliefs, since one would realize the experiments might not support the beliefs. What further suggestions for introducing openness can you draw from other fields, such as literary studies or home economics or your own favorite?

**3.** Or, in a more positive vein, academic subjects and roles can be used to facilitate open consideration of other people's ideas—that is, to decrease certainty that others are wrong. Awareness plans such as **building on others' ideas and looking for points of agreement with some aspect of others' ideas** can obviously be of service here. Simply ask how a particular type of specialist might build on the other person's ideas or what types of possible agreements the specialist might suggest. A role based on simple arithmetic, say, might lead to thinking of constructive ways to borrow from others' ideas (as in subtraction or long division) or perhaps to searching for the lowest common denominator underlying your own and the other person's ideas. Meteorology might lead to advice such as looking for what kind of brainstorm you can precipitate by swirling your own and the other person's ideas together (what would follow if you tried saying both sets of ideas had to be true?). Such use of academic roles to help build on alternative ideas and find agreements can be rather challenging, but the payoff in creativity and open-mindedness can be substantial.

## Constructing Mind-Opening Lesson Plans

All of the sample lesson plans in this book show ways in which academic content can be used to enhance mental flexibility, a key ingredient in open-mindedness (and creativity). However, there are special challenges in constructing lesson plans that specifically address the process of widening students' windows of uncertainty and their latitude of openness to others' ideas. Here are a few ingredients we suggest for your consideration:

**NOTES**

**NOTES**

1. Engage students in dialogue with each other on hot topics about which they have held strongly opposing beliefs or about which they all strongly agree with each other. In the former case, students can be encouraged to exchange beliefs with each other and then use academic content or thought patterns (specialist roles) to look for value in the other person's position or to build on it constructively. Alternatively, if the students start out in agreement, they can collaboratively explore the possibility and implications of being wrong (again using curricular content to bolster their thinking, as suggested by the various awareness plans presented in this chapter).

2. Involve the students in treating their own and others' ideas and values in much the way art criticism proceeds. This process involves carefully examining and analyzing a work of art (or, as we are suggesting, a set of ideas) *before* forming a definite opinion about its value or how much one likes it. What a contrast with how most of us normally go about reacting to art or ideas! The underlying awareness plans in art criticism seem to involve noticing what is there, figuring out what its intention or function is, evaluating how well it fulfills that function, and possibly thinking up alternative suggestions. (See, for example, Feldman 1992.) Such an approach can provide a productive framework for building on others' ideas, critically examining one's own, and also using academic content and roles as analytical and creative resources.

3. In the case of disagreements, actively encourage students to work toward creative, dialectical synthesis of conflicting ideas or toward building consensus in some other creative way. If students adopt the goal of genuinely resolving and actually benefiting from conflicts—rather than of setting out to

"win" them—they will be much more receptive to each other's ideas. A good warm-up activity for this is the "great artist" collaboration exercise mentioned in chapter 4 (p. 117). This activity affords excellent practice in treating others' ideas with respect and inclusiveness.

4. For follow-up, encourage students to use real-life disagreements and other conflicts as opportunities to extend, practice, and share their skills in open-mindedness. You might try asking them to employ specific academic roles as thought enhancers for critiquing their own beliefs, building on others' ideas, and exploring new ways to evaluate and form judgments.

## Sample Lesson Plan

**GOAL:** To use any academic content to increase open-mindedness

**PROCEDURE:**

*Step 1:* Ask your students to brainstorm areas about which they want to be more open-minded. List the ideas on newsprint or on the blackboard. Select the "hottest" or most frequently mentioned topic to use for this lesson.

*Step 2:* Place students in groups of three or four. Assign each group to an artificial position, either for or against a selected topic. (Half the groups should be pro and half con.)

*Step 3:* Give a set time (say, ten minutes) for each team to formulate its position. They should imagine that they start out *absolutely sure* that the team's position is right.

*Step 4:* Pair each pro group with a con group and ask the two groups to discuss their positions with each other for about five minutes—all the time holding on to the feeling of absolute certainty about the correctness of their original positions.

**NOTES**

*Step 5:* Now split the teams again, and ask each team to take about ten minutes to see how they might introduce at least a sliver of doubt about their original position. They can start by asking how specialists in subjects they are studying might go about questioning their position, or asking what alternative positions such specialists might propose they consider. Point out to the teams that success here means *decreasing* their original absolute certainty. (Each group should assess its success before going to the next step.)

*Step 6:* Again pair each pro group with a con group. This time, ask the combined groups to build on each other's ideas and to look for areas of actual or potential agreement. As discussed earlier in this chapter, encourage them to use academic specialist roles to help find ways to integrate the originally opposing ideas, to seek some common ground, or even to form a totally new position on which the original teams agree.

*Step 7:* Ask each student to do a five-minute free-writing reflecting on what she or he experienced and learned during the different steps of this activity.

**EVALUATION:** Check to see if the class is more open-minded about the topic they worked on (and about any of the other original issues they mentioned). Also assess with the students how well they were able to use academic roles to help open their window of uncertainty and to forge integrated new positions with the originally opposing teams. Which roles seemed to help the most? Why? Where did the students seem to need more information in order to make effective use of the associated academic roles? Notice if individuals or teams used any back-up resources (for example, dictionaries or textbooks) to formulate their positions. Check to see if the class wants a special lesson on any specific subject matter in order to make fuller use of roles or ideas derived from it.

**FOLLOW-UP:** Discuss with the students how they might use some of the processes of the exercise to increase their own open-mindedness or to encourage other people to be more open to alternative ideas.

You might try allowing them to role-play some of these situations and to advise each other on possible strategies and on constructive new uses for academic roles based on curricular content. Also check with the students a week or ten days later to see if they've actually used any of these ideas or noticed any changes in their open-mindedness. And by all means suggest they make a follow-up entry on open-mindedness in their journals!

**NOTES**

## An Example

Here, in his own words and those of his students, is how one teacher adapted and used our sample lesson plan. Although he substituted everyday roles related to the topic for straight academic roles, his adaptation—and the responses of his students—clearly point up the value of both open-mindedness as a goal and the process of this activity as a means.

### *Using the Open-Mindedness Lesson Plan*

by Robert Rock, Hunt Middle School,
Burlington, Vermont

**SETTING:** Two teachers and forty-five seventh- and eighth-grade students completed this lesson during Enrichment Period, which typically covers a variety of topics such as literature, writing skills, computer literacy, and adolescent psychological development (drugs, alcoholism, human sexuality, and peer relationships with friends and family).

**OBJECTIVE:** The students needed to practice the skills of tolerance and respect for other people's opinions.

*Step 1:* Instead of having the students brainstorm areas they wanted to be more open-minded about, I selected the issue of hand gun control because I knew the students were evenly divided on the issue. There were no complaints from the students about the assignment. (This may be an indication of open-mindedness in itself!)

*Step 2:* I assigned students to groups of four or five and assigned each group a pro or con position. As an initiation to the team assignment, I explained the objective of being open-minded. Students enjoyed being told that they were learning a very sophisticated adult reasoning process.

*Step 3:* Teams were given ten minutes to brainstorm and record all the possible arguments to support their assigned pro or con position. I encouraged them to list all the reasons they could envision for their position, even if they didn't completely agree. Most groups listed at least five reasons to support their group's stance on gun control.

*Step 4:* I asked each group to meet with a group having a different viewpoint from its own. I asked the groups to avoid debating (arguing) and instead to elaborate the reasons for their respective positions. Groups were encouraged to record all the positions presented by the opposing groups. At this point, some students overtly displayed no sense of tolerance for their opponents' opinions. They quickly tried to shout down their opposition. I was quite busy assuaging their passion and informing them that constructive debates on their positions would be possible in a few minutes (after they had first listened and paraphrased the opposition). This explanation seemed to satisfy the more vocal students and perhaps for the first time in their lives they learned that open-mindedness means letting the other side at least say its point of view without being shouted down or humiliated. Students at least listened.

*Step 5:* I introduced specialist roles for students. I had noticed that many struggled to listen and appreciate the opposition's position. The specialist roles were intended to facilitate their taking another viewpoint. Specialist roles included police officer, lawyer, hunter, doctor, judge, gun manufacturer, arms dealer, child, gun collector, woman, man, gun lobbyist, clergy, gun victim, gun shop owner.

I spent a few minutes explaining how the roles might help students think up ideas for supporting their positions and starting to understand their opponents' positions. A student for gun control was shown how a gun shop owner might feel differently about the issue; a student opposed to gun control was shown how the family of a shooting victim might feel. I could see the students grasping the connections. Now each group was to list some reasons why positions originally opposing their own could be at least considered. Each group listed at least one opposing specialist role and created supporting opinions based on it.

*Step 6:* Students again met with opposition groups to see if now there was some common ground for discussion and consideration, and perhaps ways to compromise or to resolve their positions. I was impressed that this time there was not a single act of overt yelling or put-down among the groups. In fact several groups reached a very quick consensus that perhaps a waiting period of several days for a person to receive a hand gun would be an excellent way to keep criminals, psychopaths, and drug dealers from getting guns. But honest citizens who might want a gun for a variety of legal reasons would still be able to obtain one.

*Step 7:* I asked students to do a five-minute free-writing for homework to express their opinions on the exercise. Many students expressed opinions similar to the following:

> *What I learned was that people always have a different opinion about guns. Also I learned that there are some good reasons why people have guns and some people don't.*
>
> (Nathan, 8th grade boy)

> *I learned that being open minded can do you a lot of good in life. You can hear both sides of the story and can make a better decision.*
>
> (Justin, 7th grade boy)

> *I learned that it's easy to be open-minded and to negotiate on almost any subject. It would make the world better if everybody could be open minded on every issue in the world.*
>
> (Jennifer, 8th grade girl)

> *I am usually open-minded, but it was really helpful to me after seeing each side of the story. The exercise is one to be used for all ages because in life you need to see both sides of the issue. If you want to really support your opinion, you must understand both sides.*
>
> (Courtney, 8th grade girl)

Many students described how their opinions on gun control had really not changed as a result of the exercise, but the students now had a better idea what it was like to be a victim of a gun crime. Or to be a hunter and really defend the right to own any type of hand gun.

I told the students this was the whole point of the lesson—to see that people from different backgrounds often have different opinions about issues. I praised the whole class for being able to sit with their peers and listen to ideas that were different from their own. I emphasized that this was an important part of being an open-minded adult.

I believe the students really benefitted from the use of specialist roles. Many students described how helpful it was to consider what a hunter, gun lobbyist, police officer, or gun victim might say about the use of hand guns. I could see that the students were motivated, and if I'd scheduled more time, they would have consulted resources such as textbooks, newspaper articles, and so on as back-up references for supporting their opinions. However, many students, especially those who own guns, had a lot of background information that they shared with their teams.

What particularly pleased me about this lesson was seeing the increased willingness to listen to others' opinions. The students expressed this attitude in their written feedback—that being open-minded about any topic is a more responsible and mature way for adults to act.

> *What I learned from this unit is that if you are open-minded and listen to the other side and compromise on issues, you will accomplish much more than just arguing over it.*
>
> (Eric, 7th grade boy)

> *Yesterday I learned how to be open-minded and compromise about something that two or more people totally disagree on.*
>
> (Marie, 8th grade girl)

**FOLLOW-UP:** I intend to pursue more open-minded lessons with this class as we discuss topics such as drugs, sexuality, and peer relationships. These students need to be in situations where they are allowed to play the role of people who have ideas and opinions different from their own. I intend to check with these students periodically to determine if they are using the skills of being open-minded in their out-of-school lives—the real value of turning education inside out!

---

Now, what are some of *your* ideas for lessons, units, or even asides or questions that could help students use academic learning and roles to boost open-mindedness (either for themselves or for people they know)?

# Summary Awareness Plan Map

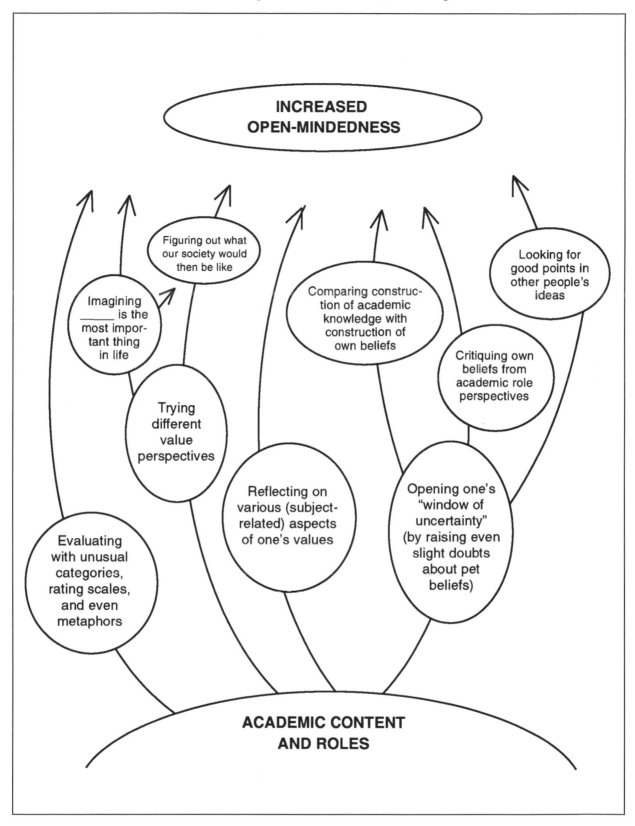

# 6

# Learning for Basic Enlightenment

How might every part of the curriculum contribute to enjoying life fully? How might learners use the content of any subject to empower themselves to treat any situation constructively—to derive or create value from it, whatever the circumstances? What special ways of thinking (APs) best help subject content contribute to such thriving?

## Basic Enlightenment

In other writings (see especially Leff 1984) we have used the term *basic enlightenment* to refer to ways of thinking and acting that would optimize the quality of life experience—that would infuse life with as much joy and fulfillment as is possible. This concept actually poses a question: What is such an optimal mode of interpreting and dealing with the world? We must be quick to admit that our answer, presented in this chapter in the form of various awareness plans and their elaborations, is offered more as a guess or hypothesis than as proven fact. Nonetheless, we do think it is a good guess, resting on both the accumulated wisdom presented in many books and psychological enrichment programs (see suggested readings at the end of the next chapter) and on our observation of the power of these plans for ourselves and our students.

## NOTES

# Using Academic Subjects to Optimize Experience

As in past chapters, the awareness plans discussed here are offered as vehicles for applying academic content to life in creative new ways. We now turn to some examples of awareness plans intended to carry subject-matter applications into the realm of basic enlightenment.

## *Generating Opportunity Everywhere*

What if we treated every situation as holding hidden opportunities—realizable potentials to add value to our lives and experience? How might we approach life differently if we deliberately (or spontaneously) adopted this orientation, especially in trying times? How might we use various creativity plans (such as those in chapter 2) to help us figure out new opportunities? What new opportunity themes or specific ideas might we derive from academic content of various types?

An essential feature of this awareness plan is to view your current situation, whatever it is, as a resource. Your circumstances, including your own feelings and reactions as well as the external situation, provide the starting place and the raw material for opportunity creation. The underlying attitude is "This is what I have to work with; now what can I constructively make of it?" The AP that emerges is probably best stated as: "Figuring out opportunities for _____ (whatever situation or situational elements you choose)."

As a warm-up, try listing possible opportunities that you might find or create for the following types of circumstances (keeping in mind that the idea is not just to think positively but to come up with meaningful ways to use the circumstances to add value to life):

**Working while feeling ill**

**Being nervous when speaking to a group**

**Grading a huge pile of term papers**

**Teaching when unprepared**

**Failing a test**

**Getting fired or divorced**

**Gaining unwanted weight**

**Being unable to figure out an opportunity**

_____ (your choice)

The listed circumstances were chosen to represent times most of us view as negative, but the Opportunity Plan can be applied to neutral and positive times as well. What are some new or alternative opportunities you can think of for events such as taking a walk, being in love, reading a novel, receiving an honor, or teaching when you are prepared?

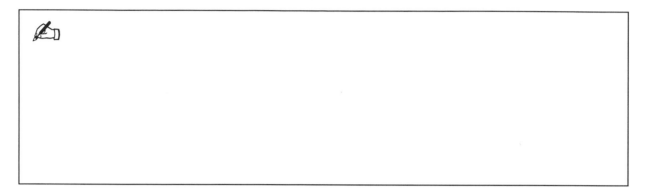

At the very least, the Opportunity AP can help you break through complacency even in the best of times.

It should be clear by now that this awareness plan calls for considerable creative thinking. You have to *figure out* opportunities for many situations; they will not necessarily be obvious. Thus, creativity assists can be very useful, and one of the best is (you guessed it) drawing on ideas and thought patterns from various academic subject areas. Following are a few examples of how this can work.

Let's start with something easy, such as taking a walk. What opportunities might a historian suggest for this? (Perhaps to reflect on your past successes, to entertain yourself by imagining what your surroundings might have looked like fifty or a hundred years ago or how a person from those times would view the current condition.) Turning to physics, what does the concept of gravity suggest? (Maybe to exult in your ability to move "against" it or in its ability to hold you close to Earth despite your momentum, or maybe to make a game out of avoiding abrupt drop-offs, or maybe to find something "weighty" to think about and resolve on your walk.) What opportunity suggestions come to mind from the following subject areas?

**Geology**

**Poetry**

**Your favorite novelist**

**Mathematics**

**Health studies**

**Some specifics from subjects you teach**

Now, for a bit more challenge, let's look for opportunities in working while feeling ill. What opportunity suggestions might a political science or social studies specialist propose? (A few possibilities: Use this situation as a chance to congratulate yourself for your good citizenship in your organization, as an opportunity to firm up your skills of leadership over your body, or perhaps to take heed of the "lobbying message" from your body concerning undue stress to which it is being subjected.) Or what suggestions for opportunity generation might Charles Dickens offer? (Perhaps a chance to develop empathy for down-trodden people who must struggle and work regardless of their health, or a chance to gather some interesting story ideas based on your new, illness-generated perspective?)

If you're game, try picking an issue for which you would genuinely welcome "opportunity ideas" and see what suggestions you can derive from the following academic roles and concepts:

**Biologist**

**Robotics specialist**

**Art historian**

**Social skills teacher**

**Sports analyst**

**The concept of osmosis (used metaphorically if you like)**

**Two or three of your favorite authors, subjects, or concepts**

## Some "Opportunity Plan" Variations

Using subject matter to generate opportunity ideas often can be aided by narrowing down the type of opportunity sought. Here are some of our favorite academically amplified variations on the Opportunity AP:

- **The Learning Variation:** Use academic content or roles to suggest what or how you can learn from any situation. For instance, mathematical thinking might suggest learning about the boundaries, limits, or grouping patterns of a situation. The field of language skills might suggest learning from anything written in the situation. The role of an ecologist might lead you to try learning from interconnections within the situation or perhaps from how that situation fits into your whole life context. Chemistry might suggest trying out some experiments or some new combinations as an aid to learning.

No matter what happens, it is always possible to learn something from it, and academic roles and subjects can provoke helpful new approaches to learning. What ideas for learning from a situation that currently concerns you can you derive right now from a subject or skill area you teach?

**NOTES**

- **The Action Variation:** Draw on subject areas or roles to generate ideas for constructive actions you can take in _____ (whatever situations you choose). So often, people regard themselves as the victims of their circumstances and think about what is being done to them rather than focus on what they can do. Of course, it is certainly useful to assess impositions and opposition you face (for which the above Learning Variation can indeed be helpful). But also regarding situations—and even impositions—as opportunities for constructive actions can add tremendously to the quality of life. Indeed, just thinking of yourself as a doer rather than a victim can make a big difference in your morale.

And curricular content—any curricular content—can be a fruitful starting place for suggesting new types of action. For instance, as we hinted in some of the examples for the Learning Variation, different subjects can suggest things to do in order to learn more from any situation (science: conduct "experiments"; English: write down your feelings or reactions; and so on). As discussed in chapter 2, academic roles and subjects are also a fertile source of creative ideas for any goal, including thinking up actions. Biology might suggest actions based on the ways different types of plants or insects behave. Social studies might lead to action ideas based on political or historical figures—as in the case of a teacher who advised her students to consider giving Patrick Henry–style speeches to persuade their parents to do something. Every academic field provides new action models in some form.

**Note:** An especially useful approach to generating ideas for constructive action is to ask what your "future self" would want you to do right now. You can pick any future time you like, from yourself at the end of your life to yourself in the next few seconds. To use academics, ask what each subject area might suggest you do to please your future self.

- **The Meta-AP Variation:** Regard any situation as an opportunity to create and use academically enhanced awareness plans. Just as the Action Variation uses academic content as a resource for developing constructive things to do, this variation funnels subject areas and specialist roles into generating useful new ways to think and to focus attention. This whole book is of course about doing just that, so we offer the current variation on the Opportunity Plan as a reminder that every situation really does offer an opportunity to use academic learning to enrich everyday thinking and experience.

## New Meanings for Wealth

In our culture, "wealth" usually signifies financial or material possessions, but other meanings are possible and may help us appreciate and orient our lives in constructive new ways. A particularly enriching way to apply academic content to life is to use it to suggest new interpretations of wealth.

Table 6-1 presents some of these academically based suggestions. You might try reevaluating how rich you are (or might become) by asking just how wealthy you would be if you substituted these alternative meanings for the usual one. And, of course, we cordially invite you to add still more alternatives to our list—and to think up a lesson or two around this theme to try with your students.

**Table 6-1**
**Some Alternative Meanings of *Wealth***

**SOCIAL SCIENCES**

*Anthropology:* Contact with other cultures

*Geography:* Places visited

*Psychology:* Density of "flow" (intrinsic satisfaction) in life; repertoire of useful APs

*Sociology:* Friends, family

*Economics:* The good one has produced in life

**NATURAL SCIENCES**

*Physics:* One's ability to *radiate* joy, *attract* other people, or add *electricity* to life

*Biology:* Health, vitality

*Chemistry:* One's ability to combine cooperatively with other people

*Geology:* Degree of passion and change ("hot lava," "tectonic movements") in one's life, or amount of stability and persistence

**HUMANITIES**

*English:* Comedy in life, drama in life

*Philosophy:* Degree one has considered "deep" issues of truth and reality; one's philosophy of life

*Languages:* Vocabulary; fluency in foreign languages (and foreign cultures)

*History:* Richness of memories

**ARTS**

*Visual arts:* Sights seen; visual awareness; beauty one has created

*Music:* Musical repertoire; sonic appreciation and experience; harmony in life

*Dance:* Fluidity and grace in life

*Cooking:* "Spiciness" or "sweetness" of life; balance in life

**Your Additions**

## *Focusing on the "Half-Full" Part of Life*

The familiar observation that you can see the glass as half full or half empty can be a very empowering reminder of how easily you can influence your outlook and feelings. Here's a simple way to demonstrate this to yourself:

First, check your mood—up, down, or neutral.

Second, ask yourself what you could focus on in life that goes against your current mood—thus, if you are feeling happy, ask what you would focus on if you really wanted to feel blue (say, if someone holding a gun ordered you to "wipe that smile off your face").

Third, focus on these "counterthoughts" to find out if you actually can start to shift your mood. (*Caution:* If you are shifting down, we advise you to cease as soon as you feel your mood genuinely start to drop; you might then reverse mental gears and start focusing as if the person with the gun decided you'd better smile after all—and really mean it!).

This particular awareness exercise is extremely useful for realizing your potential to influence your own emotions. Of course, most of the time you would likely want to use it to increase good cheer in life rather than to make yourself miserable. Ironically, though, even realizing that you can make yourself miserable by conscious choice empowers you, since you then know that you can direct your feelings. The catch, it seems, is that at some level we often want to feel the way we do, even when that's rotten. Feelings, after all, are messages; it pays to look beyond the immediate joy or distress to find out what those feelings are telling us. Nonetheless, there are times when it is both safe and sane to nudge ourselves into a more spirited, serene, or otherwise pleasant state.

The simplest and best trick we have yet discovered for mood elevation is to start by asking yourself, what if you *had* to feel happier; what would you focus on (or do)? (Mind you, it's important to tell yourself that you don't really have to do whatever the answer is; the point is just to alert yourself to some possibilities.) This awareness plan—disguised here as a question— will almost always yield some answers, because in fact life's glass really is *partially* full most of the time.

**NOTES**

Some things you value will be going well, and some not so well, at any particular time. The important thing is to realize how many different types of things you actually value. It is hard to keep all those aspects of our values in focus at one time; usually most of us concentrate on just a few areas—often those that are going wrong. And here is where academic content can come in very handy.

Academic subject areas, with their wondrously rich conceptual networks, can help remind us of those areas of life and values that we might overlook, especially when we are stuck in a rut. The previous awareness plan's use of academic content and roles—to figure out alternative meanings of *wealth*—can be a good starting place. For each meaning of wealth, try ferreting out all the places in your life where that interpretation would make you "rich."

Another approach is to imagine that you have an inner consultant or even an inner guru from the particular subject area. What would this consultant suggest to help you achieve an emotion you target? For example, to increase serenity, an "inner guru" from mathematics might suggest focusing on all the ways things balance out in your life. An inner biological consultant might recommend meditative focusing on your heartbeat or breathing, or contemplating the biological rhythms that flow through life. Or, if you are striving for a sense of joy, a historian consultant might suggest surveying all the happy moments you can remember. Where might a geographer point you in your search for the "half-full" portion of life?

Or a physicist guru?

And how about some of your favorite authors or characters from literature as inner advisers?

The possibilities are clearly as broad as one's knowledge. What a treasure each new area of academic familiarity would become if it helped to open our minds to the richness that we already possess in our lives.

## New Meanings for Self

Another especially empowering way to use curricular content is to generate ideas for new ways to think of oneself. This "self"-focused variation of the Metaphor Plan (see chapter 3) is worth singling out because of its power to help people reframe and redirect creatively their whole approach to life. Let's explore this with some simple examples drawn from a variety of subject areas:

Try thinking of yourself as
a ratio, square root, exponential function

```

```

a capital, continent, natural resource

```

```

a verb, exclamation, question

```

```

a statistician, astronomer, experimenter

```

```

a poet, novelist, essayist (and hence your life as a poem, novel, essay)

a painter, composer, dancer

Now, how far can you develop each of these academically generated self metaphors? First, what new awareness and action plans does each suggest? For instance, thinking of yourself as a ratio might lead you to focus on the relative proportions of various components in your life. Regarding yourself as an exponential function might help you notice ways in which you can greatly magnify the value or use of your skills and tools. Thinking of yourself as a poet or composer creating your life as a work of art can be an especially inspiring metaphor for taking your life into your own hands and for appreciating yourself as a creator. And notice how various artistic styles may then become very useful to understand, as each one can suggest whole new approaches to interpreting or creating your life.

To continue, what new interpretations—"reframings"—can each self metaphor call forth for your feelings, goals, and actions? Thinking of yourself as a statistician, for instance, could lead to your treating emotions as helpful messages about your probability of your achieving various outcomes in life. The self metaphor of astronomer could suggest viewing your feelings or goals as sources of energy and light. And the metaphor of dancer might lead you to think of your actions and emotions as . . .

Finally, what new ideas arise from combining some of these metaphors? For example, what new ideas for constructive actions, awareness plans, and self-interpretations are suggested by such combined self metaphors as a "poetic statistician," a "sociological chemist," or even a "dancing square root"? (Let's see: If we view ourselves as dancing square roots, we think about aligning the underlying concerns in our lives—the "square roots" of our surface concerns—with the movement and rhythms of our circumstances. As "sociological chemists," we focus on building empowering and beneficial teams—"social compounds"—with other people.) What are some of your ideas for such composite self metaphors?

What potential class or homework activities might you build from this way of using academic roles and concepts?

## *Imparting Significance and Celebration Everywhere*

Perhaps the ultimate contribution academics might make to basic enlightenment would be to help us regard whatever we are doing and experiencing as somehow deeply meaningful and even as a celebration. In a playful vein, the Holiday Plan (chapter 3) tapped into the spirit of this goal, but there are ways to go still further.

The core awareness plan we have in mind is **to figure out why (or how) whatever you are doing or experiencing might be deeply significant and a celebration (or perhaps even, in some sense, sacred)**. Academic content can then be used to help suggest creative possibilities. Let's delve into some examples to explore how this can work.

Take the case of children playing at recess. It's easy to see this as a celebration of body movement, games, and the spirit of fun. What are some possibilities for deeper significance as well? Psychology, for instance, might suggest viewing such play as a pure form of intrinsic motivation or as a primary expression of what Robert White (1959) called "effectance motivation"—possibly the driving force behind human learning and creativity. Physics might lead us to view recess play as a celebration of momentum or the bioelectrical processes that enable the children to make such complex movements. What reasons for significance and celebration might you derive from something you teach?

For a bit more challenge, what basis for significance and celebration might we find in enforcing school rules concerning behavior? Anthropology might suggest reveling in one's ongoing participation in a human culture. Geometry could lead to finding significance in following rules and in the logical reasoning required to recognize infractions. Botanical metaphors might lead to finding rich meaning and value in the act of "sowing seeds of responsibility." What ideas come to mind based on subjects you teach?

As a final example, consider a serious issue such as divorce. What advice or new perspectives might some academic disciplines offer for meaning and celebration even here? What comes to mind for, say, computer science? (Perhaps growing beyond an obsolete life program? Or . . . ?) What might various literary figures suggest? (For example, Feodor Dostoevsky: the deep significance of human conflict and suffering? Mark Twain: the adventure of major life changes, or perhaps the opportunity to find wry humor in difficult times? One of your favorite writers:_____?) And what new suggestions for significance and celebration might arise from specific concepts, such as radioactivity (the creation of two new "nuclei" for potential new families from the fission of an old one?), revolution (the sweeping away of an outmoded regime, or perhaps the celebration of human struggle for "freedom"?), or a special topic you love to teach?

In the next chapter, we explore ways to use subject matter to grasp interconnections and to stimulate integrative and cooperative approaches to other people and the environment at large. These approaches also support the kind of personal basic enlightenment discussed in this chapter, and they add especially to the awareness plan of figuring out why (or how) one's actions and experience might be significant and celebrational. Before launching on that grand journey into holistic thinking, however, let's conclude with a sample lesson plan integrating several approaches to our current theme of basic enlightenment.

## Sample Lesson Plan

**GOAL:** To use curricular content to help develop skill and creativity in taking a highly constructive, positive, basically enlightened approach to life

**SAMPLE PROCEDURE:**

*Step 1*  (3 minutes): Ask your students to list situations in their lives that they would like to approach more constructively—perhaps things such as schoolwork, outside jobs, or dealing with their families.

*Step 2*  (5 minutes): Give each student one of the awareness plans discussed in this chapter (1 = Opportunity Plan; 2 = Wealth Plan; 3 = "Half-Full" Plan; 4 = Self Plan; 5 = Celebration Plan) and ask them to think about what would happen if they approached life that way all the time.

*Step 3*  (5 minutes): Ask the students to free-write on how an expert or specialist in the subject matter you are teaching would advise them to use their assigned awareness plan to approach their situations more constructively. You might even suggest that each subject specialist be thought of as a kind of "inner guru," so that students can then turn to their inner "math guru" or "history guru" for wise advice.

*Step 4*  (8 minutes): Pair students who received two different APs, and ask the partners to teach each other how to apply the subject matter (the specialist role) through their respective awareness plans. Each pair should also use these academically enhanced APs to give each other advice on their respective situations.

*Step 5*  (10 minutes): Form student foursomes by pairing groups that had diverse APs, and ask each group to explore together how to apply subject matter through all four awareness plans represented.

*Step 6*  (10–15 minutes): Give each group a chance to tell the whole class about any especially promising or interesting ideas that emerged, with special emphasis on how the subject matter helped. (To add liveliness and memorability, you might also suggest that the groups create ads or skits to present their ideas.)

*Step 7*   (5 minutes): Ask students to write down the ideas and content applications they found most promising from the various presentations.

**EVALUATION:** You might collect the final summaries of promising ideas as a way to check on the apparent value of the activity, again paying special attention to whether curricular content is actually being used. In addition, though, you can ask the whole class to give feedback and further suggestions concerning the use of actual academic content to enrich life. The class can also be asked to supply verbal or written feedback on the exercise itself and how it might be improved or elaborated.

**FOLLOW-UP:** As suggested in prior sample lesson plans, students can be asked to tell or write about actual use of any of the ideas generated during the exercise. They can also be encouraged to try the same approach with other subject areas, to share resulting ideas with other people (outreach), and to report on how all this works out. Since basic enlightenment as defined in this chapter is such an empowering goal if it is seriously pursued, such follow-up encouragement would seem extremely worthwhile.

We realize this lesson as presented is fairly complex—but it does show a way of integrating several basic-enlightenment awareness plans, use of academic roles with each plan, application to students' own concerns, and cooperative learning processes (not to mention ads and skits!) into a single class activity. How would you adapt or revise this lesson plan for use in your own class (pretending perhaps that someone with a gun has ordered you to come up with some things you might actually do!)?

# Summary Awareness Plan Map

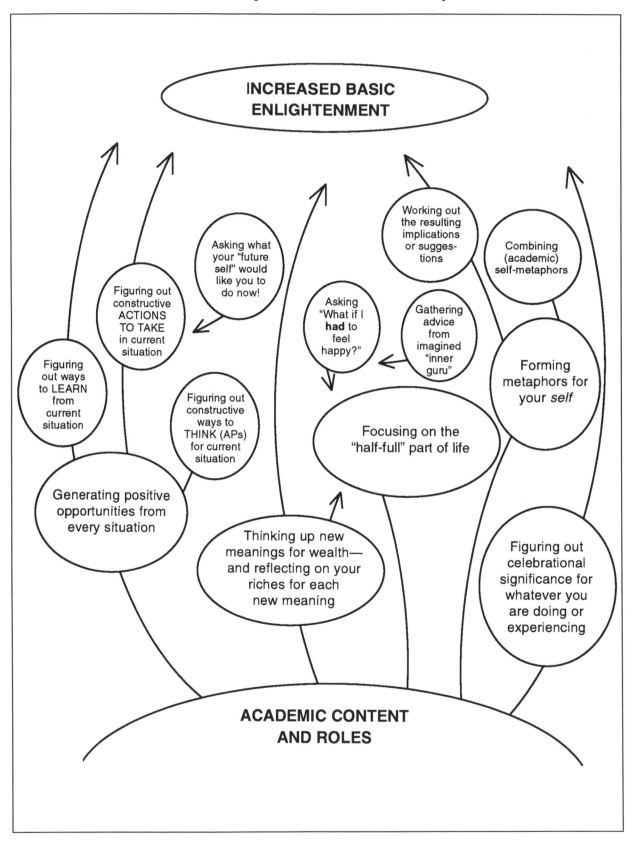

# 7

# Learning for Synergistic Thinking

How can curricular content contribute to an understanding and appreciation of the deep interconnectedness of all things? How might such holistic thinking in turn contribute to more harmonious and constructive social relations? What are examples of awareness plans and educational procedures for empowering learners to use academic roles and subject matter for these synergistic purposes?

## Interconnection

It is becoming a commonplace idea that everything is connected to everything else. The world seems to "shrink" almost daily, as events in apparently remote places fan out, at least through the news media, to affect our everyday life and thought at an increasing rate. Ecology continues to teach us that we are very much a part of our environment—and vice versa. And if we stop to think about it, it is quickly apparent that the people in our lives help to define the very essence of our being—and we do the same for them.

Given that everything, including ourselves, really is interconnected with everything else, what follows? In part, the realization of our interconnectedness can itself be a source of comfort and perhaps even a cause for celebration. Drawing from Eastern philosophy,

**NOTES**

writers such as Alan Watts (1966) have provided hints of the joys of recognizing that in a deep sense, each of us *is* the universe. All conscious creatures can indeed be thought of as the universe experiencing itself. That idea can certainly impart some significance to anyone's existence.

On a more practical and mundane level, realizing the pervasiveness of interconnection can pave the way for a much more cooperative and empathic stance toward other people and toward the natural environment. Such an orientation can be of enormous value for our social and environmental well-being.

We could of course argue the point further, but it seems a good bet that enhancing understanding and a sense of interconnection would be a very empowering and constructive application for academic content. Before turning to some special awareness plans to facilitate this application, let's briefly explore the broader goal we have in mind.

## Synergistic Thinking

*Synergy* refers to the power of combined action, especially where the resulting power is greater than a simple summing of the individual components acting alone. Everyday examples include the combined effects of certain drugs or foods, the way individual frames in a movie combine to create the illusion of motion, and the power of cooperative learning and problem-solving processes to enhance participants' enjoyment and success.

*Synergistic thinking* thus takes on an instructive (and perhaps synergistic) ambiguity. It can refer to thinking *about* synergistic combinations, or to thinking that *produces* synergistic ideas (ideas that lead to synergy), or to thinking that *results from* synergistic combinations with other thinking. All three meanings represent worthy goals to which academic content and thought patterns can be applied. These goals are worthy because each not only fosters a focus on interconnection, but also promotes a cooperative building on ideas. As noted in chapter 2, combining ideas and striving to derive value from any idea are powerful assists to creativity. Building on others' ideas is also a powerful aid to social well-being and interpersonal encouragement.

## Using Academic Subjects to Think More Synergistically

What are some specific awareness plans that can facilitate the use of academic content for such holistic, synergistic, "interconnectionist" thinking?

### Contemplating One's Total Situation

One of the easiest and most accessible holistic ways to use academic subject areas is to help realize the range and richness of one's "total situation." First, though, try thinking of all the domains of your own current total situation. What comes to mind?

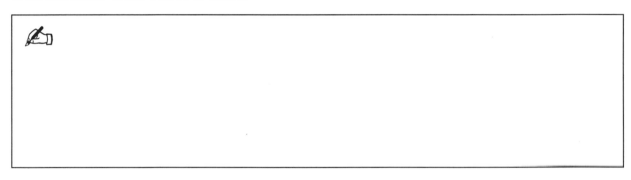

(Perhaps you thought of the people in your life, the world of your work, the information environment created by mass media, your immediate physical surroundings, the Earth as a whole and its position in the astronomical realm, and so on.)

What role do you play in each aspect of this situation (even in the astronomical realm)?

Now, to see how academics can be extremely useful in extending the range and detail of your understanding of your total situation, simply plug in subject areas or even specific concepts, as follows: **Contemplate the _____ (subject-specific) aspects of your total situation.** For instance, what are the *historical* aspects of your situation? Or, phrased another way, what aspects of your situation would a historian be interested in?

What are some *geological* aspects of your situation (a good way to focus on the ground beneath your feet as well as on the impact a major earthquake in, say, California could have on your life)?

What aspects of your situation do your own areas of teaching or interest highlight?

Even seemingly esoteric subjects can provide new insights about your situation: What are some Eastern philosophical aspects of your total situation?

What role does parallel versus serial information processing play in your life (such as in the operation of computers—or our own brains)?

What light can quadratic equations throw on your situation (perhaps turning to word problems in algebra for some ideas)?

What would a specialist in American Indian cultures point out about the context of your life?

Since all academic areas deal in some way with the world in which we live, learning about new subjects provides a wonderful resource for gaining new insight into our overall situation. Each new domain of academic content thus offers the potential to enrich learners' appreciation of the fabulous variety of ways in which they are interconnected with the world. What are some potential class activities or assignments you could incorporate to help your students gain this appreciation within the subject areas you teach?

## Forming Possible Superordinate Goals

A *superordinate* goal is one that draws individuals or groups together to work toward it. Such goals help people overcome divisions and transcend their idiosyncratic personal concerns to join in a common effort. Examples include community members uniting to clean up and rebuild after a natural (or social) disaster, or a class pulling together to stage a play or a party. Even the process of searching for possible superordinate goals can be extremely synergistic, since finding a true superordinate goal requires gaining an understanding of other people's underlying needs or desires and is greatly facilitated by cooperative and creative thinking with other people.

Since formulating superordinate goals calls for considerable creativity and breadth of social understanding, academics can supply a particularly useful set of resources. The enhanced awareness plan here is **to figure out possible superordinate goals suggested by various academic subject areas or roles**. Following are some examples of how this can work.

Let's say you're looking for goals to unite and excite a group of fellow teachers. What ideas might the literary genre of science fiction suggest?

(From the associated idea of robotics, you might think of, say, the goal of automating some of the drudgery involved in school record keeping or grading. From the idea of life on other planets, you might think of planning a foreign tour for the whole group or perhaps a faculty costume party.)

What candidates for superordinate goalhood might a mathematician offer?

(Perhaps group construction of some sort of "proof" that composes a cogent argument for why a strongly felt need among the faculty should be met. Or perhaps a composite—additive—set of individuals' goals that would promote the formation of a teacher coalition.)

What suggestions can you derive from a topic you are about to cover in class?

Or let's try devising some possible superordinate goals for a group of schoolchildren. What might a specialist in twentieth-century history suggest?

(Maybe that students pool their resources or put on a joint rummage sale to buy a high-tech game or toy they could all share, or perhaps that they somehow mimic the United Nations by forming a club for their mutual emotional support and protection.)

How about a specialist in African geography?

(Maybe putting together a play on the plight of African elephants to present to parents or fellow students, or making up their own role-playing adventure game based on an African culture.)

Drawing on a subject area you have taught recently, what suggestions might you offer your students for superordinate goal candidates?

What classroom activities might help the students derive their own ideas for superordinate goals by drawing on roles inherent in your subject matter?

**NOTES**

A somewhat more analytical approach to using subject areas is to ask what each can suggest for improvements in life and then use those ideas as starting points for possible superordinate goals. Arithmetic might suggest adding or subtracting things from life to improve it and hence lead you to look in that direction for possible superordinate goals. Biology might suggest various types of health-related improvements. Physics could lead you to think of the pooling of energy or the decrease of friction (conflict) as areas for life enhancement and thus superordinate goal possibilities. Or, to get more specific, you might explore how particular authors or subspecialists would suggest improving life and go from there. Hermann Hesse might suggest a religious resurgence, for instance; a Renaissance historian might advise a flowering of the arts; and so on. Each academic area or role can sow our thinking in new and fertile ground from which possible superordinate goals could spring.

Still another way to use academic content to suggest possible superordinate goals is to call on some of the academically enhanced awareness plans from earlier chapters. Especially useful might be plans such as the Holiday AP (chapter 3), through which subject areas and roles can generate ideas for special celebrational themes. Examples such as "Catalyst Day" from chemistry or "Appreciate Citizens of Other Countries Day" or "Local Color Day" from geography can readily give rise to possible superordinate goals for a class. Superordinate goal ideas can also be drawn from APs such as using subject matter to create games (Game Plan in chapter 3), to generate interesting questions (chapter 4), or to suggest new meanings for wealth or new types of opportunity (chapter 6). Indeed, to the degree any subject-enhanced awareness plan leads to ideas worth pursuing, it can provide a conduit from curricular content to possible superordinate goals.

It is important to keep in mind, though, that a goal is superordinate only when people concur in viewing it as more important and worth pursuing than their individual goals. Just because a goal is exciting and preeminent for oneself does not necessarily mean it will draw comparable enthusiasm from other people. The only way to find out is to check with the other people. One of the best preliminaries for figuring out superordinate goal candidates is thus to figure or find out other people's underlying needs and desires. It also helps a great deal to work *with* the other people to generate possibilities. An excellent classroom application of the superordinate goal idea is to have students work in cooperative groups and ask them first to locate some important needs or desires they have in common, then to use curricular content or specialist roles to help them think of possible class projects to fulfill one or more of these shared wants.

## Building on Others' Ideas

As mentioned in chapter 2, one of the most empowering ways to nurture both creativity and interpersonal harmony is to focus deliberately on how to use or build on others' ideas rather than to focus on what is wrong with them. How can academic subject matter assist in finding constructive uses for ideas that seem hard to build on?

First it may help to look at some of the subplans that can support the main AP of **figuring out ways to build on ideas**. Some useful supporting awareness plans include the following:

- **Looking for points you agree with in new ideas,** even when you disagree with the idea as a whole or the argument it serves. For instance, you may disagree with the argument that because it figures prominently in Japanese education, we should rely on rote learning. But you may agree with the underlying idea that we can gain valuable insights by drawing on other cultures' educational approaches. Such points of agreement can be easy to build on.

- **Thinking of all ideas as gifts or invitations**. These are especially powerful metaphors for engendering a positive attitude toward new ideas. In fact people usually do offer their

**NOTES**

ideas as a kind of gift—an attempt to share their vision of the truth. And it is easy to treat any idea as an invitation to explore its underpinnings and implications and perhaps to build on or improve it in some way. Thinking of one's own ideas in these ways also helps bolster openness to constructive criticism and to using others' ideas to enhance one's own.

- **Thinking of agreeable transformations in ideas you disagree with**. If all else fails in searching for a way to build constructively on an idea, try strategies such as reversing the idea or perhaps exaggerating it. Reversals can at least allow you to explore some new possibilities (say, doing the opposite of whatever the Japanese do in education). Exaggeration (example: requiring all lessons to be taught in Japanese) at least offers potential for humor along with possibly useful new starting places for creative ideas (what new "languages" might really yield some valuable new educational approaches?). Other useful transformations might include weakening or qualifying the idea ("occasionally it is true that . . . "), imagining some context in which the idea would be true or appropriate, or even imagining that you won the idea as a prize or that it is a valuable work of conceptual art.

Now to return to how academics can contribute to building on new ideas, what happens if we try drawing on a variety of specialist roles? What techniques might a mathematician suggest, for instance?

(Perhaps to explore ways to add to or subtract from the idea, to divide or multiply it somehow, or to explore the premises underlying the idea to find a place to start building.)

What suggestions come to mind for a historian?

(To explore how the idea arose and build from there? To seek documentation for the idea as a possible starting point for enhancement? To ask how various historical figures might build on the idea?)

What about a physicist or chemist?

(To experiment with alterations of the idea? To try some new combinations of this idea with others?)

Or a specialist in literature?

(To use the idea as a basis for a story? To ask how various authors or literary characters might build on the idea?)

Or some roles based on the subject matter you teach?

Actually, creatively and effectively building on ideas, whether one's own or other people's, is a challenging and often difficult procedure. In our culture, academic training typically orients us toward debunking ideas but gives us much less encouragement for finding or creating value in "flawed" ideas. To build on ideas calls for both creative thinking and a shift in our stance toward our own and others' thoughts. Once we have made a commitment to look for points of value in new ideas, to think of any idea as a gift or invitation to explore, and to work with an idea to derive some value from at least a transformation of it, academic content can supply a rich resource of helpful mental roles and thought strategies. Indeed, it is precisely in cases calling for increased creativity that the conceptual and methodological richness of scholastic subject areas is most clearly useful. How might you help your students learn to use academic specialist roles to build on ideas creatively?

## Sample Integrative Lesson Plans

### Sample Plan 1

**GOAL:** To use subject matter to help increase harmony in relations with other people

**PROCEDURE:**

*Step 1*  (5 minutes): Ask the class to generate a list of the types of interpersonal or social conflicts in their lives. (An alternative is to ask the class to list larger social conflicts from the news or even historical conflicts.)

*Step 2*  (5 minutes): Ask each student to pick the type of conflict she or he would most like to work on and form small groups based on their choices.

*Step 3*  (10 minutes): Instruct the groups to list aspects of the situation in which their chosen type of conflict might occur, giving special attention to aspects that are suggested by subject matter you are currently covering in class. Also ask the groups to list probable underlying needs or desires contributing to the conflict, again drawing on subject matter and associated specialist roles to suggest probable needs. (Biology, for instance, might suggest physical needs of various sorts; geology might suggest needs arising from pressures in life.)

*Step 4*  (10 minutes): Now ask the groups to build on their ideas from Step 3—and on each group member's ideas as they arise—to form proposals for superordinate goals for those involved in the conflict. Each group is again to use curricular content and specialist roles to assist it in generating creative ideas for goals that could overcome the type of conflict the group is working on.

*Step 5*  (15–20 minutes): Give each group an equal share of time to tell the class its most promising ideas for superordinate goals to resolve its type of conflict; ask each group to indicate how it used subject matter or roles to help generate the ideas.

**NOTES**

*Step 6*   (3 minutes): Ask all students to write down the ideas and content applications they find most promising—especially any ideas they might be able to use in their own lives.

**EVALUATION:** The group reports can indicate a lot about the likely value of the activity. How many ideas did each group generate? How much curricular content seemed to be involved? Similarly, looking over the students' final free-writings can also give helpful feedback regarding how valuable the superordinate goal was to individuals in the class. As usual, you can gain additional feedback by asking the class for verbal or written suggestions about the exercise itself.

**FOLLOW-UP:** As always, a good follow-up to this type of activity is for students to report in journals or in class about any actual use they make of the ideas generated in class. They can also be encouraged to use other subject areas to help generate new ideas for understanding and resolving conflicts, drawing on the awareness plans from the exercise. Additionally, as either a follow-up or a pre-activity, you can ask the students to try using curricular subject matter or roles to generate ideas for superordinate goals for the class to work on together.

What other follow-up ideas can you think of now, perhaps tapping specialist roles from your favorite subjects to suggest some creative approaches?

### Sample Plan 2

**GOAL:** To develop skill and practice in synergistically pooling subject-area knowledge and skill for the purpose of reaching out to other people

**PROCEDURE:** Select one of the other lesson plans in this book (or a similar one of your own devising) as a starting place. After completing that activity, ask your students to form new groups to pool what they learned and thought up during the activity. Then ask each group to plan—and ultimately carry out—an outreach project to share those skills and ideas with people outside the class. Some possibilities might include writing an article for the school paper; creating a collage or poster for public display; sending letters with suggestions to friends, relatives, or appropriate officials; staging a play or musical performance that carries the message they would like to pass on; or conducting a workshop or creating an academic-applications game for other students. The outreach groups can also use specialist roles and creativity plans like those in chapter 2 to help them generate imaginative outreach projects.

This procedure can of course serve as a follow-up activity for any lesson that generates new ideas with real-life relevance. One of the most powerful and empowering ways to learn is to teach other people, and a profound source of human satisfaction (and hence superordinate goal possibilities) is making a contribution to other people. As discussed further in the next chapter, such outreach is a major pedagogical tool for both learning and empowerment.

**EVALUATION:** Journal and class reports of the outreach activities, with special emphasis on how the curricular content contributed, are good choices for feedback from the students. Checking for any indications of increased interest and mastery of the subject matter is also worthwhile as an assessment of whether higher student motivation is being engaged.

**NOTES**

**FOLLOW-UP:** Since outreach activities *are* follow-ups, we are actually thinking of "meta-follow-up" here. One intriguing possibility is to have the students encourage and help the people with whom they shared their gains do the same for still other people. This creates the potential for a rippling or even exponentially expanding outreach. Some other possibilities include encouraging your students to conduct outreach projects based on other curricular content; conducting in-class discussions about the significance and process of subject-based outreach work; holding an "outreach fair" in which students display posters, demonstrate applications games, perform skits, or otherwise vividly convey their outreach efforts; and asking the students for their own suggestions for follow-up. And, of course, what ideas would you now suggest?

# Summary Awareness Plan Map

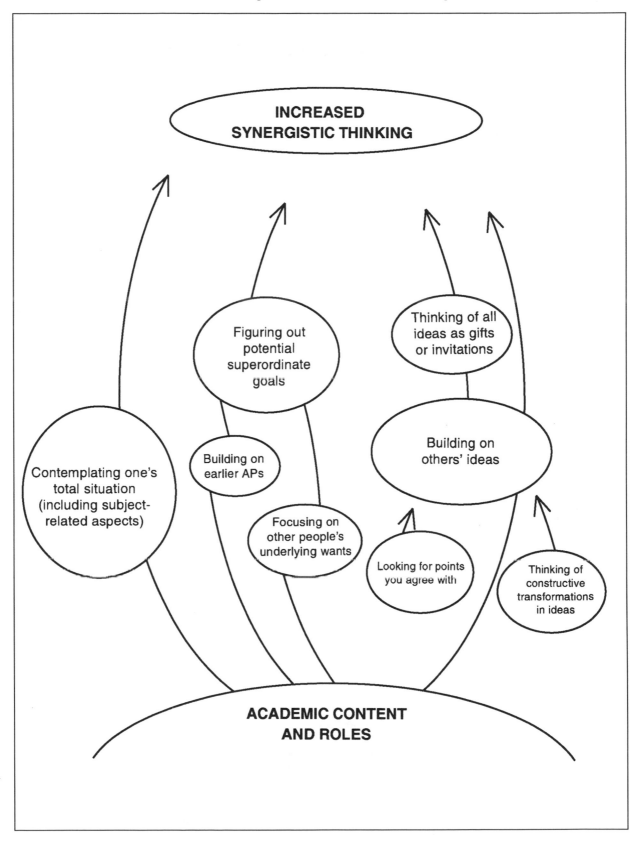

## Suggested Readings on Basic Enlightenment and Synergy

Argyris, Chris, and Donald A. Schön. *Theory in Practice: Increasing Professional Effectiveness.* San Francisco: Jossey-Bass, 1974.

> First, and still perhaps most wide ranging and provocative, in a continuing series of books by Argyris and his associates on two alternative guiding philosophies for dealing with people: the widespread "Model 1" (basically, get your own way and be in control) versus the proposed "Model 2" (share power and seek synergistic solutions).

Bach, Richard. *Illusions: The Adventures of a Reluctant Messiah.* New York: Dell, 1977.

> A short, thought-provoking novel, replete with images and messages conveying a sense of self-empowerment through the way we frame or conceive of our lives.

Bateson, Gregory. *Steps to an Ecology of Mind.* New York: Ballantine Books, 1972.

> Somewhat difficult but ultimately very enriching example of thinking in terms of interconnections, with essays spanning most of Bateson's illustrious, brilliant career in anthropology (and many related fields).

———. *Mind and Nature: A Necessary Unity.* New York: E. P. Dutton, 1979.

> A unified, book-length essay on the "immanence" of mind in nature.

———. *Sacred Unity: Further Steps to an Ecology of Mind.* New York: HarperCollins, 1991.

> A posthumous compilation of additional examples of Bateson's highly synergistic thinking.

Covey, Stephen R. *The Seven Habits of Highly Effective People.* New York: Simon & Schuster, 1989.

> A popular set of guidelines for thinking and acting in a basically enlightened and synergistic way (with a definite Western slant toward personal planning and goal directedness).

Csikszentmihalyi, Mihaly. *Flow: The Psychology of Optimal Experience.* New York: Harper & Row, 1990.

> Very clear, popularly written treatise on Csikszentmihalyi's explorations of what leads to high satisfaction in everyday life experience.

Ferguson, Marilyn. *The Aquarian Conspiracy: Personal and Social Transformation in the 1980s.* Los Angeles: J.P. Tarcher, 1980.

> A thoughtful and thought-provoking overview of synergistic transformations brewing in a very wide range of domains (including education).

Fisher, Roger, and William Ury. *Getting to Yes: Negotiating Agreement without Giving In* (2nd ed.). New York: Viking Penguin, 1991.

> A practical yet highly synergistic approach to bargaining, with the stress on searching for creative resolutions that rely on joint agreements about fairness rather than appeals to threats or other power-based tactics.

Glasser, William. *Take Effective Control of Your Life.* New York: Harper & Row, 1984.

> A behaviorally oriented approach to increasing personal self-direction and constructive living by the developer of "reality therapy" and the concept of "positive addiction."

Golas, Thaddeus. *The Lazy Man's Guide to Enlightenment*. Palo Alto, Calif.: Seed Center, 1972.

> Exceptionally light guide to constructive living; our favorite line: "when you learn to love hell, you'll be in heaven."

Gordon, Thomas. *T.E.T.: Teacher Effectiveness Training*. New York: Peter H. Wyden, 1974.

> An application of Gordon's highly synergistic "effectiveness training" approach specifically to teaching.

Houston, John P. *The Pursuit of Happiness*. Glenview, Ill.: Scott, Foresman, 1981.

> Advice for increasing life satisfaction based on various principles from psychology; especially helpful on the roles of expectation, habituation, and aspiration.

Jeffers, Susan. *Feel the Fear and Do It Anyway*. New York: Fawcett Columbine, 1987.

> Highly empowering advice for making creative use of what we have called the "Opportunity AP": treating every situation as an opportunity for learning and personal growth.

Keyes, Ken, Jr. *Handbook to Higher Consciousness* (5th ed.). St. Mary, Ky.: Living Love Publications, 1975.

> A guide to developing inner mental resources for happiness so that external situations become less of a determinant for one's feelings, or, as Keyes puts it, to turning "addictions" into "preferences."

Kohn, Alfie. *No Contest: The Case against Competition* (2nd ed.). Boston: Houghton Mifflin, 1992.

> A very lucid and persuasive look at the synergistic value of cooperation as a guiding way of virtually all aspects of social life.

Leff, Herbert L. *Experience, Environment, and Human Potentials*. New York: Oxford University Press, 1978.

> Extended discussion of the psychological theory underlying the suggestions in this book, including presentation of a theory of the key components in conscious experience that seem to underlie the quality of life.

——. *Playful Perception: Choosing How to Experience Your World*. Burlington, Vermont: Waterfront Books, 1984.

> Presentation of a wide variety of awareness plans for the enrichment of life.

Maslow, Abraham H. *Toward a Psychology of Being*. Princeton, N.J.: Van Nostrand, 1968.

> Maslow's classic treatment of the higher reaches of psychological health (self-actualization).

Myers, David G. *The Pursuit of Happiness: Who Is Happy–and Why*. New York: William Morrow, 1992.

> A popularly written account of psychological evidence on the distribution and correlates of happiness, along with some constructive advice on possible personal applications.

Nachmanovitch, Stephen. *Free Play: Improvisation in Life and Art*. Los Angeles: Tarcher, 1990.

> Eloquent advice for more creative and enjoyable improvising in virtually any domain of life or art.

Ram Dass. *The Only Dance There Is.* Garden City, New York: Anchor Press, 1974.

> Highly readable presentation of Ram Dass's (previously Richard Alpert) "be here now" philosophy; very helpful look at the psychology of Buddhist acceptance from a Western perspective.

Ram Dass and Paul Gorman. *How Can I Help? Stories and Reflections on Service.* New York: Knopf, 1985.

> An inspiring collection of accounts of people making richly synergistic contributions to the well-being of others.

Rheingold, Howard. *They Have a Word for It: A Lighthearted Lexicon of Untranslatable Words and Phrases.* Los Angeles: Tarcher, 1988.

> A delightful compendium of often synergistic and basically enlightened concepts drawn from languages from around the world; many new awareness plans can be derived from these concepts.

Ury, William. *Getting Past No: Negotiating Your Way from Confrontation to Cooperation.* New York: Bantam books, 1993.

> Excellent follow-up to Ury's earlier book with Roger Fisher, *Getting to Yes,* this time focusing specifically on ways to engage adversarial thinkers in synergistic, mutually beneficial negotiations with you.

Watts, Alan. *The Book: On the Taboo against Knowing Who You Are.* New York: Collier Books, 1966.

> Helpfully metaphorical, Westernized introduction to the Eastern notion that we are one with the universe; a genuine aid to experiencing this sense of interconnection.

# 8

# Turning Teaching Inside Out

What teaching practices and styles best support turning learning inside out? How might thinking like a learner help? What benefits occur when students take on the teaching role? How can students be helped to **teach the teacher** what's important to them? What instructional procedures mobilize students to action? What can the teacher do so that students become actively engaged in using what they learn?

Before reading further, please take a few moments to make your own list of what teaching practices—and teacher characteristics—seem most likely to help students develop the types of "inside-out" skills discussed in previous chapters.

**NOTES**

## The Inside-Out Teacher

You may have noticed that the lesson plans we've developed for each of the chapter themes change the traditional role of the teacher in two basic ways. First, the teacher is no longer the single source of information. Although there are plenty of opportunities for the teacher to give mini-lectures to set the context and procedures for the lesson, the main sources are the students themselves and their reference resources. Second, the teacher can be an active, collaborative learner along with the students in researching, discovering, and inventing solutions to the students' goals.

This means that the teacher's role is reversed in much the same way that learners assume the teacher's role when they become peer tutors. Learners as teachers and teachers as learners form a dynamic duo, leading to a continuously evolving educational experience.

***The Traditional View of the Teacher.*** Do you remember how you viewed your teachers? Were you slightly in awe of them? Did you take their word as law? Did you ever question your teachers' knowledge or statements about something? The view of the teacher as a knowledge conduit, as an infallible answer-knower, and as *the* authority in the classroom can still be found in many of today's schools.

***The Traditional View of the Learner.*** Do you remember how you were treated as a learner? Were you expected to sit still, be quiet until called upon, and do your lessons independently? Were your opinions or past experiences valued? The view of the learner as a "blank slate" and passive recipient of information and knowledge from the teacher has long been a popularly held position.

***The New View of the Learner-Teacher and the Teacher-Learner.*** The new view of learners and teachers is more reciprocal. When the give and take of teaching and learning is acknowledged, the sharp separation between who is a learner and who is a teacher dissolves, which can lead to some major educational gains. When learners assume the role of teacher, their learning is enhanced. And similarly, when teachers assume the role of learners, their teaching is enhanced. Most important, this broadening of teacher and student roles invites the kind of active cognitive involvement needed for inside-out educational applications.

### Overview of the Inside-Out Teacher: A Role Map

A role map of the inside-out teacher might look like this:

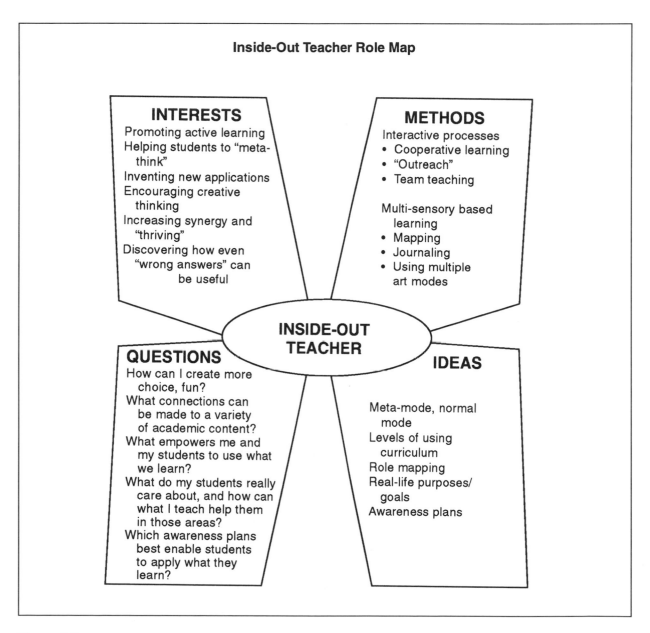

**Inside-Out Teacher Role Map**

**INTERESTS**
Promoting active learning
Helping students to "meta-think"
Inventing new applications
Encouraging creative thinking
Increasing synergy and "thriving"
Discovering how even "wrong answers" can be useful

**METHODS**
Interactive processes
• Cooperative learning
• "Outreach"
• Team teaching

Multi-sensory based learning
• Mapping
• Journaling
• Using multiple art modes

**INSIDE-OUT TEACHER**

**QUESTIONS**
How can I create more choice, fun?
What connections can be made to a variety of academic content?
What empowers me and my students to use what we learn?
What do my students really care about, and how can what I teach help them in those areas?
Which awareness plans best enable students to apply what they learn?

**IDEAS**
Meta-mode, normal mode
Levels of using curriculum
Role mapping
Real-life purposes/ goals
Awareness plans

**Figure 8-1**

**NOTES**

## The Inside-Out Teacher in Action

Inside-out teachers share their passion for ensuring that their students can use the academic content covered in school. They view students as their partners in designing and evaluating learning experiences. Being a good inside-out teacher means being willing to build on what students say is meaningful and what students say they need. The inside-out teacher is really a learner and inventor—progressively devising and modifying lessons based on what students are saying and doing.

We believe that inside-out teachers demonstrate a leadership process, showing new directions in education. When you observe inside-out teachers in action, you'll see and hear them doing things such as the following:

- **Inside-out teachers focus on how students apply academic content by letting students speak for themselves.** Students tell each other about their personal applications, thus helping establish norms for using academic content in life outside school. When students see and hear how their friends are using academic content, rather than viewing this approach as solely the teacher's way of doing things, they will be more likely to integrate such application into their lives.

- **Inside-out teachers encourage their students to think creatively.** They invite students to develop and express their own thoughts. They congratulate students when the students make creative connections. They bring quiet students out and give not-so-shy students quieter roles. They also get their students to work in cooperative groups and encourage students to build on each other's ideas (a key aid to creative thinking) and to take on the roles of peer teachers and peer consultants.

- **Inside-out teachers ask questions that result in thinking about how to apply content.** In addition to constructing special lessons around themes of meta-thinking (deliberately exploring new awareness plans) and creative use of specialist roles, inside-out teachers often throw in asides and thought-provoking questions about how to use any lesson's content to enhance creative thinking. They make such applications a recurrent, underlying theme in the classroom.

- **Inside-out teachers set up lots of choices, knowing that students are turned on by choice.** Such teachers routinely suggest several alternative assignments and a variety of ways to use the curricular content, and they invite students to come up with their own ideas for classroom activities and homework.

- **Inside-out teachers model the types of thinking and action they wish to encourage for their students.** Thus, these teachers share their own learning and thinking processes, often thinking out loud about how they might use what they're teaching to help solve problems or enrich various awareness plans. They also enjoy team teaching and openly welcome chances to cooperate with other teachers and to involve students as co-teachers whenever possible. They build on students' ideas and actively join in classroom groups during cooperative projects and activities. They also use various art forms and sensory modalities to match their students' learning styles, openly learn from their students, and are eager to try new approaches.

## Teachers as Learners

What happens when teachers take on the role of learners? Of course teachers are accustomed to the learner role—they are often the most frequent consumers of continuing education courses! However, such learning typically occurs away from the classroom. What we're suggesting here is that teachers publicly share their role as learners in such a way that their students can observe the learning strategies that teachers themselves use.

**NOTES**

**NOTES**

An especially powerful way that teachers can share their learning strategies is to think out loud with their students, showing how the teachers develop ideas for using academic content. Teachers who show their students how to use academic content as a resource for reaching goals or solving their current problems are empowering their students to use academic content actively. For instance, Rosanna Lupien, a high school science teacher, showed her students how she worked through the problem of "senioritis" by forming metaphors based on their newly acquired knowledge of the endocrine system. This example of the teacher's thinking helped the students get actively involved in using this academic material to work on other applications of interest to them.

Another empowering way teachers can function as learners is to ask their students what issues and goals are important to the students. (Actually, this also involves our next theme of students as teachers.) Recall from chapter 2, for instance, how Susan Underhill used the straightforward approach of asking her fifth graders to decide in groups what issues and problems were most important to them. The key issues were then listed on large sheets of paper that were posted in the room, thus providing a reminder for the whole class about issues worth receiving creative applications based on academic content. This information also proved valuable to the teacher in constructing future lessons that built on the students' real concerns.

As noted in chapter 2, Susan also asked her class to list the ways of thinking involved in the various academic disciplines they had been studying. The class's considerable collective insights about each role were also posted around the room as helpful reminders for future inside-out applications. Here again, the teacher took on the learner role, allowing her students to reveal their understanding both to her and to each other. Interestingly, she was pleasantly surprised at just how much her students did know about the concepts and ways of thinking of each academic specialty (math, language arts, and so on).

Teachers can also be productive inside-out learners by asking thought-provoking questions that can lead to useful new ideas being offered by their students. For instance, many of our favorite awareness plans and class activities have developed from ideas generated by our students in response to our questions and assignments. Indeed, much of the excitement and value of teaching often derives from what teachers can learn from their students. This will be especially true in classes emphasizing applications of subject matter. Even first graders can offer some wonderful ideas (for adults as well as each other) if they are set to solve problems and enrich life by using whatever they happen to be learning in school.

### Team Teaching

As a final example of the power of the teacher as learner, let's consider team teaching. The key to effective team teaching is the exchange of knowledge or practice. For example, you might choose to work with a person who has a science background and is skilled at using the Hunter Model for lessons. You, on the other hand, are skilled at the Sterns Manipulative Methods for teaching mathematics. After reviewing appropriate background material and observing each other's lessons, the next step is to schedule time for you to practice with your partner as coach.

You'll notice that team teaching is *not* sequential teaching with you in charge of the class for the first thirty minutes and your partner in charge for the next thirty minutes—this might be called tag team teaching. In essence, good team teaching means that your students experience both of you at all times.

Here are some tips from a couple of master team teachers we know.

**NOTES**

**NOTES**

## TEAM TEACHING TIPS

*Diane Happy and Karen Pearo*

- Plan carefully before teaming—ease into it (combine classes and planning for one area such as science, then expand gradually); create philosophical agreement (a common approach to discipline, math, and so on).

- Build on complementary strengths, learning styles, teaching styles.

- Communicate with parents about the teaming arrangement the semester before children are assigned; in the fall hold an open house so children can teach their parents the system.

- Clearly mark all books and items that you combine so that if administrative support for teaming shifts, you can divide with less trauma (inventory carefully).

- Operate as a team—both sign all notes, say "we" instead of "I," have joint conferences.

- Model cooperation, caring, questioning, validating answers, personal anecdotes; model the types of thinking and actions you wish to encourage in the children.

- Remember that team teaching requires more work and thought at first but is energizing and exciting, not isolating.

## Learners as Teachers

What happens when students assume the role of teachers? Informally you have probably invited your students to tutor each other, perhaps to help each other study for a spelling test. You have noticed how some students seem to be better coaches, perhaps in teaching an arithmetic algorithm or a skill in sports. Your personal observations about the benefits of peer tutoring or partner learning may be similar to the research findings (see, for example, Pierce, Stahlbrand, and Armstrong 1989). In addition to increased academic performance, benefits to the students being tutored (the "tutees") include increased individualized attention, increased contact with instructors, influence of a positive role model, and gains in self-esteem.

Researchers have been concerned about the effect on the tutor as well. Benefits to the tutors include increased understanding of the subject matter, increased self-esteem, acquisition of social interaction skills, and increased self-acceptance/awareness and tolerance of others. Learning new material with the intent to teach it to others also provides a significant boost to the original learner's enjoyment and interest in the material (see Deci 1992). In addition, the experience of being useful to others brings many undermeasured results.

When students assume the role of tutor or partner learner, what are the benefits to the teacher? Teachers who have established peer tutoring programs report they are able to ensure more individualized instruction for all their students. Low performers as well as high performers and average students all seem to benefit. "Gifted" students enjoy being able to invent effective teaching methods for their tutees. Low performers who themselves become tutors (instead of being only tutees) enjoy the role of helping others. Average students often emerge as skillful supporters of their tutees. Teachers as well as researchers have also noticed that learners' attitudes toward the subject matter often improve (see, for example, Johnson, Johnson, and Holubec 1987). In summary, teachers benefit because peer tutoring programs are a cost-effective, easily managed method of increasing individualized instruction with resulting increased academic achievement and positive attitudes toward the subject.

Why do these and other cooperative learning processes support turning learning inside out? Our approach calls for learners to choose consciously how they'll think and to make deliberate use of academic subject matter to solve problems they choose. When learners actively share their thoughts about how to use subject matter in this way, they empower each other to forge new applications for the material they are learning *and* they get better at solving problems. Students learning in partnership also have more

**NOTES**

interactions with each other. The center of attention is the active learner. In addition to increasing retention of academic subject matter, cooperative, active learning is associated with higher levels of cognition, problem solving, and group cohesiveness—all of which support meta-thinking and active use of academic knowledge.

### *Steps in Organizing and Managing Partner Learning Programs*

For details on how to set up partner learning and peer tutoring programs, see Pierce, Stahlbrand, and Armstrong (1989); Cooke, Heron, and Heward (1983); and McNeil (1994). It has been demonstrated that formally organizing your peer tutoring program will lead to better, more consistent and reliable results than the informal methods that are usually followed. Table 8-1 shows the outline of steps recommended by Pierce and her colleagues.

**TABLE 8-1**
**Steps in Organizing and Managing Tutoring and Partner Learning Programs\***

1. **Choose the Partners and Select Goals**

   Learning objectives
   Personal goals

2. **Design the Program with the Following Essential Curriculum**

   Pre-established sequence of instructional objectives
   Measurement and monitoring system
   Pretests that lead to instructional prescriptions
   Posttests that check mastery
   Appropriate instructional materials
   Clearly delineated teaching/learning methods

3. **Train the Peer Tutors**

4. **Monitor the Peer Tutors and Their Tutees**

   Celebration of accomplishments
   Troubleshooting procedures

5. **Evaluate**

   Regularly scheduled intervals
   Recommendations for redesign

\*From Mary Pierce, Kristina Stahlbrand, and Suzanne Armstrong, *Increasing Student Productivity through Peer Tutoring Programs,* Monograph 9(1), 6–10. Burlington, Vt.: Center for Developmental Disabilities Monograph Series, University of Vermont, 1989.

## *Heterogeneous Cooperative Groups*

When your students learn in heterogeneous cooperative learning groups, thus engaging in cooperative learning (CL), you may notice two major outcomes. First, your role will shift dramatically; because the students will be relying on each other, you'll be a facilitator and a coach rather than the dispenser of information. Second, the way that students interact with each other will change as they acquire and practice the social skills necessary to communicate effectively and resolve the intellectual controversies they experience about what they are learning.

The good news is that CL is easy to learn. The challenging news is that it takes time to become comfortable with the changes in your role and in the students. The "8 Steps of the Teacher's Role" shown in table 8-2 can be an effective tool in creating CL lesson plans. (This summary table is based on the work of David and Roger Johnson and their associates. See, for example, Johnson, Johnson, and Holubec 1987.)

**TABLE 8-2**
**The 8 Steps of the Teacher's Role in Cooperative Learning***

1. **Select an Academic Instructional Objective and Materials**

2. **Select the Group Size and Assign the Students to Groups**

3. **Arrange the Classroom in Clusters**

4. **Set the Cooperative Goal Structure**
   (Goal-Reward-Resource Interdependence)

5. **Specify the Criteria for Success**
   (for both the academic task and the social interactions)

6. **Monitor Groups and Individuals**

7. **Intervene When Necessary**
   (to teach the academic or social skills)

8. **Evaluate**
   (both the academic and social interactions)

*For more information about cooperative learning workshops and sample cooperative learning lesson plans, write Judy Bartlett, National Cooperative Learning Center, Pattee Hall, University of Minnesota, Minneapolis, MN 55455.

**NOTES**

As you know, there are three ways you can orient your students to achieve their goals, and each way leads to certain interactive patterns between you and the students. For example, let's say you give the class a spelling lesson that requires them to learn twenty words. If you orient them *individualistically,* they must learn the words on their own. The expectation is for each student to work alone, perhaps at individual work stations. If you orient them *competitively,* each must learn the words faster or more accurately than others in the class. They're expected to compete, and you might see them forming coalitions of same-ability groups to practice. If you orient them *cooperatively,* they're expected to learn their own words and to support others in their group to learn also.

Beware of what Roger Johnson calls "the fuzzies"— assignments that look like or sound like cooperative learning but aren't. For example, the competitive or individualistic spelling assignment described above can become a "fuzzy" if you add, "It's okay for you to work with a partner." Basically, fuzzies are confusing to your students and often lead to confusing results and less than optimal learning.

You can structure cooperation by varying how you organize achieving academic goals. Through *goal interdependence* you require a single product from each group (perhaps a worksheet or poem or story) that reflects the work of each person in the group (individual accountability). When you structure a lesson using *resource interdependence,* you make sure that each person in the learning group has a responsibility for a specific amount of the content (another way to ensure individual accountability). When you use *reward interdependence,* the entire group receives the same consequence, perhaps a grade or a privilege.

You'll notice that you can use CL for all sorts of activities. Almost any instructional objective will be better attained when your students learn in a predominantly cooperative classroom. CL works best when you assign students heterogeneously rather than homogeneously so they can capitalize on each other's diverse learning capabilities, opinions, and needs. Because this diversity often leads to challenges, you'll notice that, in addition to teaching the academic objectives, your students will be directly practicing several important social interaction skills. Even if you don't teach the social skills directly, your students will use them as they form their groups, function in the groups, and formulate strategies to accomplish the group's task.

## *Outreach*

Every teacher is well aware that teaching is one of the best ways to learn. Giving your students chances to teach others is thus a very empowering aid to their own learning. Peer tutoring, partner learning, and the interactions in cooperative groups illustrate some of the possibilities. Student presentations in class and student-designed lessons and exercises are other useful approaches (see the next section). Perhaps the most useful of all, in terms of relevance to real-life applications, is what we call "outreach"—the process of students passing on their learned ideas and skills to people outside the classroom.

One of our favorite procedures for setting up outreach projects was discussed at the end of chapter 7 as Sample Lesson Plan 2. This process consists essentially of asking students first to reflect on the skills and insights they have gained from a particular lesson or unit (or whole course or year, if you like), and then to figure out ways to pass these gains on to other people. The actual outreach, of course, is for the students to carry out one or more of their ideas for sharing their learning with other people. (As noted in the lesson plan in chapter 7, this might consist of such activities as writing letters or school-paper articles, creating message artwork for public display or performance, conducting workshops for friends or students in other classes, and so on.)

This process has several benefits. Since students first reflect on the ideas, insights, and skills they have learned, they are more likely to integrate their new knowledge and skill and to appreciate their own cognitive growth. Thinking up ways to share these gains also helps to solidify the learning and to provide a focus for real-life applications. Even if particular students have no pressing personal applications for

NOTES

**NOTES**

themselves in mind, they may well know someone else who *could* benefit from their new knowledge or insights. Assisting other people to deal more effectively with their own goals and problems enables the original learner to function at the top level of the applications balloon (see figure 1-1). Moreover, making such contributions to other people tends to be both intrinsically satisfying and a boost to the helper's self-esteem (see *How Can I Help?* by Ram Dass and Paul Gorman [1985] for some fascinating and instructive case studies of helping). Finally, outreach projects of this sort can be an excellent source of truly superordinate goals (see chapter 7) for everyone involved.

In addition to taking on full-scale outreach projects, our students have found it very beneficial to do "mini-outreaches." These can be as simple as a casual word of advice to a friend or asking a helpfully thought-provoking question in another class. The key is for the student to use mindfully something she or he has learned to help someone else think more effectively. If each learning experience is approached with the underlying intention (and associated awareness plan) to *think of how it could be used to benefit other people as well as oneself,* all of education can become an adventure in prosocial living.

### Student-Generated Activities

Finally, a most beneficial way to involve students as teachers is to invite (or require!) them to develop actual lessons and in-class activities and exercises to help each other learn. For instance, we have found that students can convey very effectively the essence and value of books to each other. We might assign a choice of multiple books and then team up students who read the same book. We usually get the class first to discuss what they want from a good presentation or activity. Then each team makes up an activity for the whole class that "gives their book away"—that helps others get inside the book and derive an understanding of its essence and insights and how its ideas might be useful for students' concerns and goals. We have found that this is an extremely efficient and engaging way for students to cover and appreciate a number of books very quickly.

Of course, students can be invited to participate in lesson design in a number of ways. Suggestion boxes, free-writings, playing teacher (very effective in kindergarten, one teacher found to her surprise), mock conventions and other role-plays, and all sorts of group presentation formats provide ready examples. The key is to invite the students to engage and involve each other in ways that really bring the academic content to life and that help demonstrate application possibilities that are genuinely meaningful to the students.

For student-generated activities, we have found the following guidelines very helpful to share with the students:

---

## GUIDELINES FOR ACTIVITIES*

1. The activity should allow the participants to experience directly what you want them to learn rather than just telling about it. You might call this process "walking the talk."

2. The activity should require active participation. All the participants should be engaged all the time.

3. The activity should be easy to explain.

4. The activity should integrate academic content *and* mental processing (thinking).

5. The activity should lead to an outcome immediately useful to the participants.

6. Time should be allowed at the end of the activity for reflection and discussion about what was learned and what its potential value is.

7. The activity should be *fun* (or at least very interesting!).

---

*These guidelines are based on the five principles of playfulness discussed in chapter 3 (see also Leff 1986). As applied to activity design, these principles are as follows: *power*—the activity should make a real difference to the participants; *permission*—the activity should give the participants permission to be playful and creative; *proaction*—the activity should encourage conscious choice and planning how to think; *proliferation*—the activity should be self-regenerating, engaging enough that participants will apply what they learn elsewhere; and *practice*—the activity should enable the participants to try out new skills and practice using new ideas.

---

## Multisensory Processes

Multisensory instructional processes consciously tap into our human sensory system for storing, processing, and accessing information. Eric Jensen (1988), the innovative cofounder of SuperCamp, the nation's most successful accelerated learning program for teenagers, suggests that the "easiest way to change your students' behavior is to change their state" (p. 21). The three most distinguishable states are visual, auditory, and kinesthetic. When students are in the visual state, they are more active, process pictures and movies, and spell better. In the auditory state, students listen better and talk more. And students in a kinesthetic state are usually doing things, touching, handling, and holding.

Before reading further, try the following experiment with yourself.

Given a large cube that has been cut into 27 smaller cubes (like a Rubik's cube) and painted green on the outside, how many of the smaller cubes will be painted:

on three sides? on two sides? on one side? on no side?

Now think about how you approached the problem-solving process. Did you close your eyes and visualize the cube? Did you draw a picture? Did you talk or mumble to yourself? Did you make a model of the box, coloring the outside? How you approached the problem-solving process is an indicator of your learning strategy for this type of task. If you visualized the cube or drew a picture, you probably have a preference for the visual state. If you mumbled to yourself, you may be predominantly auditory. And if you needed a concrete model, your preferred strategy is probably kinesthetic.

**NOTES**

When academic content is matched to sensory state and students' personal learning strategies, learning and achievement are accelerated. However, when mismatches occur, learners often appear unmotivated and "stupid." When teachers expand their lessons to include directions and instruction capitalizing on state and strategy, mismatches are decreased.

**The Visual State.** In any class, *some* students will prefer to learn visually—looking at, reading, being shown, or watching. Visual learners like puzzles and neatness, and they often use expressions that are visually related (for example, "Picture this," "See what I mean?" or "I have a new perspective"). Good spellers use a predominantly visual strategy. Visual learners appreciate handouts, diagrams, and charts to guide their learning. Idea maps, concept maps, and role maps are good strategies to enhance the visual state (see the section on idea maps below).

**The Auditory State.** Other students in a class will prefer to learn auditorially—listening, talking with others, talking to themselves, and so on. Auditory learners enjoy reading aloud, singing, and knowing the words to songs. They use auditorially related expressions (for instance, "That sounds good," "I hear you," or "Something tells me to be careful"). Auditory learners respond well to lectures, discussions, and audiotapes. Of course auditory learners will be good at "sounding out" words and may find that such a strategy does not lead to success in spelling. Thus they may need to learn visual strategies.

**The Kinesthetic State.** Still other students will likely prefer to learn using the kinesthetic or tactile sensory mode—handling models, manipulating objects, touching and feeling. Kinesthetic learners like to move more slowly through a lesson, feeling their way through their experience. They use expressions such as "How does that feel?" or "I grasp the basic concept." Kinesthetic learners blossom when teachers arrange experiential learning activities such as playing sports, making things, acting things out, and doing hands-on experiments. They too can benefit from strengthening their visual and auditory strategies.

**NOTES**

### Journal Writing

The process of journal writing is an example of a combined kinesthetic and visual activity. When you ask your students to write spontaneously (or free-write), their patterns of thinking about the topic are revealed. Toby Fulwiler (1987) describes the successful efforts of teachers who use free-writing activities and journals to expand their students' thinking (and writing) across varied curricular material—one way to promote interdisciplinary learning.

Journals and free-writings can be used to focus students on the task (for instance, to describe what they observe during a series of experiments), to assess what students understand about a topic (say, before and after a lecture or a unit), to develop and share their understanding (such as when they exchange their free-writings and incorporate each other's ideas in rewrites), or to generate further topics to teach (for example, when the journal entries reveal that students have a misconception or a desire to learn something more about a topic). Perhaps one of the most exciting outcomes is when students reflect on their own journal entries, discover what gaps they have in what they know, and then search for information on their own.

Moreover, journals can be a powerful resource for generating personally meaningful applications of subject matter, academic roles, and awareness plans. For instance, you can quickly introduce and practice new awareness plans and academic applications by asking students to do journal entries or to free-write on questions guided by the awareness plans (for example, "What themes for new holidays could be suggested by our spelling words this week?" or "What questions might a mathematician ask about your favorite game or hobby?"). The students' written reflections and answers for such questions can also form the basis for other multisensory activities, such as artwork, skits, rap songs, and the like. Any productive classroom experiences such as these can extend outward into the students' lives—and even into others' lives through the students' outreach activities.

Despite the many benefits of student journals, reading and giving feedback on them can turn into a fairly time-consuming, albeit very interesting, task for the teacher. Some possible solutions are (1) to ask students to exchange journals and give feedback and advice to each other before turning them in to you (thus freeing you simply to read over the journals and make more global or selective comments), (2) to ask students to highlight the parts of their journals they deem most important or that they desire comments on most (or perhaps ask students to hand in only key excerpts from their journals), or (3) to spot read sample journals rather than read all of each student's work.

Even if students keep journals only for themselves and never turn them in, the process of writing down one's thoughts is so valuable that we hope you will encourage it in some form for all your students. One lesson we and our students have learned repeatedly is that even a great idea can be lost easily if it doesn't get written down. Another lesson, a little less obvious, is that writing down one's thoughts and experiences can *lead* to great ideas.

### Idea Maps

Idea maps are diagrams or other visual representations of concepts, propositions, questions, awareness plans, or other types of thoughts. This is a particularly powerful tool for visual learning, creative thinking, and applying awareness plans. As we saw in chapter 1, role maps (a particular type of idea map) can be extremely useful for analyzing and surveying the concepts and ways of thinking in any academic area. Diagramming of this sort can also be very helpful for developing insight into interrelations among subject areas or for figuring out how various roles can enhance awareness plans. Another benefit is the opportunity for students to combine visual art and writing.

Joseph Novak and Bob Gowin (1984) have researched the use of concept maps, which they call a "technique for externalizing concepts and propositions"

**NOTES**

**NOTES**

that fosters creativity. Such maps are also helpful in identifying gaps or misconceptions about what the learners know, thus helping teachers guide their instruction. John Clarke's (1990) book, *Patterns of Thinking,* provides an especially useful and wide-ranging look at different types of academic "graphic organizers"—visual schemes for representing ideas and thought patterns. Tony Buzan's (1983) book, *Use Both Sides of Your Brain,* and Nancy Margulies's (1991) book, *Mapping Inner Space,* as well as her video (1994), *Maps, Mindscapes, and More,* are also excellent resources for idea-mapping strategies.

### Other Multisensory Tools

Just about any art or craft mode can also provide innumerable ways to enrich learning. For instance, we have found it very enlivening to combine artistic expression with learning academic content by asking our students to create skits, ads, or music to show what they have learned and how their learning can be applied. This combination adds excitement and flair to the lesson, helps students shake up their thought processes (step 1 in creativity plans, as discussed in chapter 2), and capitalizes on nonverbal methods of expression. It also offers the opportunity to engage all three states—visual, auditory, and kinesthetic.

Table 8-3 presents what we fondly refer to as "The Matrix" and shows how various art modes can be integrated with the modes of creative, life-enriching thinking discussed in this book. The Matrix also indicates how academic content and roles can be integrated as a "third dimension" for the table. Each example illustrates how an art mode can be integrated with the academic enhancement of a life-enriching awareness plan. To see how you can use this process in your own teaching, try filling in some additional examples.

(An effective approach is to start with an awareness plan from the chapter of this book that fits the thinking mode theme you would like to help your students use. Then generate a question or assignment that would get your students to apply roles based on your subject content to help in using that awareness

## TABLE 8-3
## Activity Matrix*
## Creativity and Art across the Curriculum

**CREATIVE THINKING MODES**

| ART MODES | Creative problem solving | Playful thinking | Appreciative thinking | Open-minded thinking | Basically enlightened thinking | Synergistic thinking (Curricular content) |
|---|---|---|---|---|---|---|
| *Visual arts* | | | E.g.: Use a math approach to draw something a particular author or literary character would especially like about you (or like about ______). | | | |
| *Movement* | | | | | E.g.: Create a dance showing constructive actions that a geographer might suggest for a situation that's troubling you | |
| *Sound* | E.g.: Make up a song based on "what if" questions a historian might pose to help you deal creatively with a personal (or social) issue. | | | | | |
| *Drama* | | | | | | E.g.: Act out skits showing a scientific approach to figuring out the underlying needs of people embroiled in a conflict of concern to you. |
| *Creative writing* | | E.g.: Write a poem about how a biologist might turn studying into a game. | | | | |
| *Mixed modes* | | | | E.g.: Create an ad combining music and drama to invite people to build on each other's ideas as different subject specialists would. | | |

**Note:** All examples are framed from the student's perspective

*Adapted from a similar matrix developed by Herbert L. Leff and Lynda McIntyre in 1989.

**NOTES**

plan on something the students genuinely care about. Finally, propose an activity that would get the students to use one or more art modes to communicate their subject/AP-generated ideas or experiences to other students. Each of the examples in table 8-3 was developed this way!)

### New Tools

So far this discussion has centered around what we have found to be successful and what the pedagogical research suggests. We believe that you are most empowered when you can experiment to discover what works best for you, with your students, in your unique situation. We urge you to be willing to combine some of the above "old" tools to create new ones that no one has yet invented.

Tools for assessment and learning that involve active thinking and that tap multisensory processes support inside-out education in ways that other tools cannot. For example, multiple choice tests do not typically lead to creative, personally meaningful uses of subject matter, whereas essay tests might, and journal entries or outreach projects easily can. Writing a journal entry, creating an idea map, or coming up with outreach plans gets the learner into a free association mode. The learner can relate information being learned to personal goals. Moreover, the very process of writing, mapping, or generating project ideas can help learners discover new ways to think. By writing from the point of view of academic specialists and using appropriate awareness plans students can discover new solutions as they write (or map or compose music or . . . ).

## The Net Result: "Evocative Learning"

**NOTES**

Evocative learning is the kind of learning that results in "Aha!" or even "Eureka!" experiences. Teachers and students who exchange perspectives, use multisensory tools for learning and thinking, and orient themselves toward real-life applications are likely to generate this type of learning.

One compelling outcome of inside-out teaching and learning is that your students are more likely to become self-directed learners. When students discover that anything they are learning in school can be used to help them in their out-of-school life, they will want to learn more about the subject matter in order to have more tools for solving problems.

When you implement these instructional processes, you may notice more student competence, higher student self-esteem, and better personal experiences of your own teaching. Your academic lessons may be more meaningful to your students, too. When you treat every lesson as a mind-expander that invites students to find creative applications for whatever they are learning, all academic subjects come alive.

Teachers and students can also receive at least one other welcome benefit when they use evocative learning procedures. We have found that when students have more commitment to learning, more passion and excitement during lessons, and more creativity and ingenuity—as they typically do in evocative learning situations—both they and their teachers have more fun.

# Epilogue

# Where Might All This Lead?

As we envision it, inside-out education includes three interlocking educational forces. At the center, of course, is the metacognitive use of academic subject matter and roles—in combination with a variety of special awareness plans—to promote life-enriching goals such as creativity, playfulness, appreciation, open-mindedness, basic enlightenment, and synergistic thinking. In addition, inside-out education includes processes that promote cooperation and that enable learners to be teachers and teachers to be learners. Finally, inside-out education strongly encourages and supports outreach activities whereby students actively share these skills in life enrichment with other people.

What types of educational and social implications might we expect if all three of these inside-out forces come to be widely adopted in schools? Please do take a few moments to list your own ideas on this before reading further!

We have posed this question to groups of teachers with whom we have worked recently. Their answers reveal a broad consensus of great expectations, summarized in figure E-1. Does this list square with your own projections about where inside-out education could lead?

## Forces For and Against Inside-Out Education

"All right," you might be tempted to say, "these implications sound great, even utopian; but, realistically, can we do it?" We have asked teachers to help us analyze the opposing and supportive forces out there in "the real world," and this is what emerged (although, again, you may find it valuable to make your own lists before reading on).

### *Opposing Forces (barriers to inside-out education)*

- Fear of change

- Need to be in control (by some teachers and administrators)

- Lack of energy or motivation

- Rigid enforcement of inflexible curricula

- Requirement of "hard" documentation of success prior to change

- Lack of funding for education

## Inside-Out Education as a Force for Change

```
┌─────────────────────────────────┐
│  INSIDE-OUT EDUCATION AS         │
│  A FORCE FOR CHANGE              │
└─────────────────────────────────┘
```

**Collaborative Atmosphere**

- Students as teachers, teachers as learners
- Cooperative learning
- Multimodal expression

**Use of Academic Roles and Meta-Thinking to Enhance**

- creativity
- playfulness
- interest and appreciation
- open-mindedness
- basic enlightenment
- synergistic thinking

**Outreach**

Students empower other people to use similar metacognitive and collaborative skills

↓ ↓ ↓

### Personal implications for students (and teachers)

Increased competence and creativity (even "intelligence") for contributing to society; more dynamic, powerful thought processes

Experiencing learning as fun and meaningful; eagerness to come to school

Increased open-mindedness and compassion, along with improved communication and cooperation

Heightened self-esteem, self-control of thought and action, and overall sense of purpose and empowerment

Increased self-insight and insight for career choice

Intrinsic motivation for learning, including *life-long* learning; better long-term retention of learning

Enhanced awareness and concern for social and environmental issues

Increased enjoyment and interest in everyday activities; better stress management; less addiction; more self-expression through art

### Implications for schools and the teaching profession

Increased empowerment by teachers (and students) to shape curriculum, scheduling, and assessment (plus a likely shift to product- or portfolio-based student evaluation, with each student treated as special)

Increased cooperation among teachers; school administration a more cooperative effort by whole staff

More interdisciplinary units and teaching, with teachers bringing "expert roles" to life for students (and each other); greater variety of subjects taught

Fewer problems with student discipline; fewer dropouts

Need for more planning time

Increased questioning and initiative by students

Heightened enjoyment of teaching; overall, school a more vibrant and exciting place to teach and learn

### Broader implications for society

Over time, increased improvements in society (due to better problem-solving skills of graduating students and to outreaches and the whole outreach orientation)

Increased synergistic interconnection between schools and the rest of the community, with more community involvement in the schools and vice versa; more respect and appreciation between schools and community

Students helping their parents (through outreaches) and ultimately becoming better parents themselves

**Figure E-1**

- Bombardment with different, competing suggested educational approaches

- Kids like it (distrust of kids' preferences)

- Feelings of powerlessness, confusion, or resistance (such as thinking, "This is *old* stuff" or "I already do all this"; see also Leff and Nevin [1990] on this particular set of "barriers").

- The accusation that "it's not realistic"

### Supportive Forces

- Willingness to try new things

- Focus on what works for kids

- Desire to apply learning

- The realization that learning is supported by connecting new knowledge to real-life concerns

- Encouragement and support for teachers to take continuing-education courses

- Movements to infuse education with thoughtful problem solving

- Teaching in themes (as well as teams)

- Outside organizations (such as industry, government, or colleges) that want creative problem solvers

- Need for all people to experience "authentic work"—work of real value to self and others

What can we do with all this? Are the supportive forces sufficient to outweigh the opposing ones? Can we perhaps turn some of the apparent barriers into positive forces (say, by inviting reluctant colleagues or administrators to join in brainstorming possible ways to deal with these barriers)?

# PERHAPS MOST TO THE POINT, WHAT CAN *YOU DO NOW!?*

We are tempted to end on that last question, but we can't resist adding just a few encouraging thoughts based on what we've seen teachers do.

First, it can make a tremendous difference to team up with even one or two other interested colleagues—*at least* to share and develop ideas and provide each other moral support. Full team teaching is even better, but we realize this is not always possible.

Second, you don't have to revamp your entire curriculum or approach to teaching in order to introduce inside-out themes. It's fine to start small, perhaps with just an occasional discussion or question concerning what advice your subject matter or associated expert roles might offer for some issue that genuinely matters to your students (or to someone else, thus encouraging outreach, too). By sticking a toe in, you can gently experiment and see for yourself whether inside-out education sparks student thought and enthusiasm.

Third, as you experience success in helping your students develop inside-out skills, why not do your own outreach with colleagues? A great way to do so is simply to let them know what you've done and to enlist their aid in helping you think up new inside-out approaches and lessons. This both shares your own creative ideas and discoveries and also gives your colleagues practice in thinking along the same lines. In addition, they may offer you some great new ideas as well.

Finally, try using the types of awareness plans discussed in this book, along with whatever roles strike your fancy, to stretch your own creative problem solving, explore interesting new ways to experience a situation, or perhaps help someone else to think more constructively. Turning learning inside out can enrich life for *all* of us.

# Invitation for Feedback and Networking

We'd love to hear from you! For one thing, our primary purpose in writing this book was to invite other teachers to join us in the search for exciting ways that academic subjects can enrich everyday thinking and life experience. We dearly hope that you are taking us up on this, trying out some of the ideas in this book, and developing new ones of your own. If so, please let us know what you and your students are doing. We would especially appreciate any samples or accounts of students' actual inside-out applications of the subject matter you teach.

Ultimately, we would like to incorporate such accounts of teacher and student applications of inside-out education into a sequel to this book. We could thus serve as a clearing house for spreading the word about the endeavors of our readers and their students. This could, in turn, help to form a network of interested teachers and also inspire other teachers to experiment with inside-out approaches.

So please keep us posted. If you write to us, we'll also keep you informed about any new developments in our work or about networking possibilities. Let's turn learning inside out together.

You can reach us through Zephyr Press or through our university departments:

Herb Leff
Department of Psychology
University of Vermont
Burlington, VT 05405

(Phone: 802-656-2670)

Ann Nevin
College of Education
Arizona State University West
Phoenix, AZ 85069

(Phone: 602-543-6300)

# Appendix

# Main Awareness Plans

## Chapter 2: Plans for Creative Problem Solving

## Chapter 3: Plans for Playfulness

## Chapter 4: Plans for Interest and Appreciation

## Chapter 5: Plans for Open-Mindedness

## Chapter 6: Plans for Basic Enlightenment

## Chapter 7: Plans for Synergistic Thinking

# Bibliography

Adams, James L. *Conceptual Blockbusting*. Reading, Mass.: Addison-Wesley, 1986.

Amabile, Teresa M. *The Social Psychology of Creativity*. New York: Springer-Verlag, 1983.

——. *Growing Up Creative*. New York: Crown, 1989.

——. "Motivational Synergy: Toward New Conceptualizations of Intrinsic and Extrinsic Motivation in the Workplace." *Human Resource Management Review* 3, no. 3 (1993): 185-201.

Argyris, Chris, and Donald A. Schön. *Theory in Practice: Increasing Professional Effectiveness*. San Francisco: Jossey-Bass, 1974.

Arieti, Silvano. *Creativity: The Magic Synthesis*. New York: Basic Books, 1976.

Bach, Richard. *Illusions: The Adventures of a Reluctant Messiah*. New York: Dell, 1977.

Barell, John. *Teaching for Thoughtfulness: Classroom Strategies to Enhance Intellectual Development*. New York: Longman, 1991.

Barron, Frank. *Creativity and Personal Freedom*. Princeton, New Jersey: Van Nostrand, 1968.

Bateson, Gregory. *Steps to an Ecology of Mind*. New York: Ballantine Books, 1972.

——. *Mind and Nature: A Necessary Unity*. New York: E. P. Dutton, 1979.

——. *Sacred Unity: Further Steps to an Ecology of Mind*. New York: HarperCollins, 1991.

Belenky, Mary F., Blythe M. Clinchy, Nancy R. Goldberg, and Jill M. Tarule. *Women's Ways of Knowing: The Development of Self, Voice, and Mind*. New York: Basic Books, 1986.

Bruner, Jerome. *On Knowing: Essays for the Left Hand*. Cambridge, Mass.: Harvard University Press, 1962.

——. *Acts of Meaning*. Cambridge, Mass: Harvard University Press, 1990.

Buzan, Tony. *Use Both Sides of Your Brain*, rev. ed. New York: E. P. Dutton, 1983.

Capacchione, Lucia. *The Creative Journal*. Athens, Ohio: Ohio University Press, 1979.

Clarke, John. *Patterns of Thinking: Integrating Learning Skills in Content Teaching*. Boston: Allyn and Bacon, 1990.

Cooke, Nancy L., Timothy E. Heron, and William L. Heward. *Peer Tutoring: Implementing Classwide Programs in the Primary Grades*. Columbus, Ohio: Special Press, 1983.

Costa, Arthur, ed. *Developing Minds*. 2 vols. Alexandria, Va.: Association for Supervision and Curriculum Development, 1991.

Covey, Stephen R. *The Seven Habits of Highly Effective People*. New York: Simon & Schuster, 1989.

Csikszentmihalyi, Mihaly. *Beyond Boredom and Anxiety: The Experience of Play in Work and Games*. San Francisco: Jossey-Bass, 1975.

——. *Flow: The Psychology of Optimal Experience*. New York: Harper & Row, 1990.

de Bono, Edward. *The Mechanism of Mind*. New York: Simon & Schuster, 1969.

——. *Lateral Thinking: Creativity Step by Step*. New York: Harper & Row, 1970.

——. *Six Thinking Hats*. Boston: Little, Brown, 1985.

Deci, Edward L. "The Relation of Interest to the Motivation of Behavior: A Self-Determination Perspective." In K. Ann Renninger, Suzanne Hidi, and Andreas Krapp, eds., *The Role of Interest in Learning and Development* (43–70). Hillsdale, N.J.: Lawrence Erlbaum, 1992.

Deci, Edward L., and Richard M. Ryan. *Intrinsic Motivation and Self-Determination in Human Behavior.* New York: Plenum, 1985.

Edwards, Betty. *Drawing on the Artist Within.* New York: Simon & Schuster, 1986.

Feldman, Edmund B. *Varieties of Visual Experience,* 4th ed. New York: Abrams, 1992.

Ferguson, Marilyn. *The Acquarian Conspiracy: Personal and Social Transformation in the 1980s.* Los Angeles: J. P. Tarcher, 1980.

Finke, Ronald A., Thomas B. Ward, and Steven M. Smith. *Creative Cognition: Theory, Research, and Applications.* Cambridge, Mass.: The MIT Press, 1992.

Fisher, Roger, and William Ury. *Getting to Yes: Negotiating Agreement without Giving In,* 2nd ed. New York: Viking Penguin, 1991.

Fogarty, Robin, David Perkins, and John Barell. *The Mindful School: How to Teach for Transfer.* Palatine, Ill: Skylight Publishing, 1992.

Franck, Frederick. *The Zen of Seeing.* New York: Vintage Books, 1973.

Fulwiler, Toby. *The Journal Book.* Portsmouth, N.H.: Boynton Cook Publishers, 1987.

Gardner, Howard. *Frames of Mind: The Theory of Multiple Intelligences.* New York: Basic Books, 1983.

———. *Multiple Intelligences: The Theory in Practice.* New York: Basic Books, 1993a.

———. *Creating Minds: An Anatomy of Creativity Seen through the Lives of Freud, Einstein, Picasso, Stravinsky, Eliot, Graham, and Gandhi.* New York: Basic Books, 1993b.

Getzels, Jacob W., and Mihaly Csikszentmihalyi. *The Creative Vision: A Longitudinal Study of Problem Finding in Art.* New York: Wiley Interscience, 1976.

Glasser, William. *Take Effective Control of Your Life.* New York: Harper & Row, 1984.

Golas, Thaddeus. *The Lazy Man's Guide to Enlightenment.* Palo Alto, Calif.: Seed Center, 1972.

Gordon, Thomas. *T.E.T.: Teacher Effectiveness Training.* New York: Wyden, 1974.

Gordon, William J. J. *Synectics: The Development of Creative Capacity.* New York: Macmillan, 1961.

———. *The Metaphorical Way of Learning and Knowing.* Cambridge, Mass.: Porpoise Books, 1973.

Hofstadter, Douglas R. *Gödel, Escher, Bach: An Eternal Golden Braid.* New York: Basic Books, 1979.

Houston, John P. *The Pursuit of Happiness.* Glenview, Ill.: Scott, Foresman, 1981.

Jeffers, Susan. *Feel the Fear and Do It Anyway.* New York: Fawcett Columbine, 1987.

Jensen, Eric. *Superteaching: Master Strategies for Building Student Success.* Dubuque, Ia.: Kendall/Hunt, 1988.

Johnson, David, Roger Johnson, and Edythe Holubec. *Circles of Learning.* Edina, Minn.: Interaction Book Company, 1987.

Keyes, Ken, Jr. *Handbook to Higher Consciousness,* 5th ed. St. Mary, Ky.: Living Love Publications, 1975.

Koberg, Don, and Jim Bagnall. *The Universal Traveler*. Los Altos, Calif.: Crisp Publications, 1991.

Koestler, Arthur. *The Act of Creation*. New York: Dell, 1964.

Kohn, Alfie. *No Contest: The Case against Competition*, 2nd ed. Boston: Houghton Mifflin, 1992.

Kreitler, Hans, and Shulamith Kreitler. *Psychology of the Arts*. Durham, N.C.: Duke University Press, 1972.

Kuhn, Thomas S. *The Structure of Scientific Revolutions*. 2nd ed. Chicago: University of Chicago Press, 1970.

Lakoff, George, and Mark Johnson. *Metaphors We Live By*. Chicago: University of Chicago Press, 1980.

Langer, Ellen J. *Mindfulness*. Reading, Mass.: Addison-Wesley, 1989.

Leff, Herbert L. *Experience, Environment, and Human Potentials*. New York: Oxford University Press, 1978.

——. *Playful Perception: Choosing How to Experience Your World*. Burlington, Vt.: Waterfront Books, 1984.

——. "Principles of Playfulness." *Creative Living* (Summer 1986): 21–25.

Leff, Herbert L., Lawrence R. Gordon, and James G. Ferguson. "Cognitive Set and Environmental Awareness." *Environment and Behavior* 6 (1974): 395–447.

Leff, Herbert, and Ann Nevin. "Overcoming Barriers to Creative and Meta-Thinking." *Teacher Education and Special Education*, 13, no. 1 (1990): 36–39.

Leff, Herbert L., Ann Nevin, Donald W. Meeker, Jeanine Cogan, and Gary Isenberg. "Turning Psychology Inside Out." In John H. Clarke and Arthur W. Biddle, eds., *Teaching Critical Thinking: Reports from across the Curriculum* (193–202). Englewood Cliffs, N.J.: Prentice Hall, 1993.

Margulies, Nancy. *Mapping Inner Space: Learning and Teaching Mind Mapping*. Tucson, Ariz.: Zephyr Press, 1991.

——. *Maps, Mindscapes, and More*. Tucson, Ariz.: Zephyr Press, 1994.

Maslow, Abraham H. *Toward a Psychology of Being*. Princeton, N.J.: Van Nostrand, 1968.

McNeil, Mary E. "Partner Learning." In Jacqueline Thousand, Richard Villa, and Ann Nevin, eds., *Creativity and Collaborative Learning: A Practical Guide to Empowering Students and Teachers*, 243–59. Baltimore: Paul H. Brookes, 1994.

Miller, George A., Eugene Galanter, and Karl Pribram. *Plans and the Structure of Behavior*. New York: Holt, Rinehart and Winston, 1960.

Myers, David G. *The Pursuit of Happiness: Who Is Happy–and Why*. New York: William Morrow, 1992.

Nachmanovitch, Stephen. *Free Play: Improvisation in Life and Art*. Los Angeles: Tarcher, 1990.

Neill, A. S. *Summerhill: A Radical Approach to Child Rearing*. New York: Hart, 1960.

Nelson, Thomas O., ed. *Metacognition: Core Readings*. Boston: Allyn and Bacon, 1992.

Nevin, Ann, and Herbert L. Leff. "Is There Room for Playfulness?" *Teaching Exceptional Children* 22, no. 2 (1990): 71–73.

Novak, Joseph D., and D. Bob Gowin. *Learning How to Learn*. New York: Cambridge University Press, 1984.

Osborne, Harold. *The Art of Appreciation.* New York: Oxford University Press, 1970.

Perkins, David N. *The Mind's Best Work.* Cambridge, Mass.: Harvard University Press, 1981.

——. *Knowledge as Design.* Hillsdale, N.J.: Lawrence Erlbaum, 1986.

——. *Smart Schools: From Training Memories to Educating Minds.* New York: The Free Press, 1992.

Pierce, Mary, Kristina Stahlbrand, and Suzanne Armstrong. *Increasing Student Productivity through Peer Tutoring Programs.* Burlington, Vt.: Center for Developmental Disabilities, Monograph 9, 1989.

Prince, George M. *The Practice of Creativity.* New York: Macmillan, 1970.

Ram Dass. *The Only Dance There Is.* Garden City, New York: Anchor Press, 1974.

Ram Dass and Paul Gorman. *How Can I Help? Stories and Reflections on Service.* New York: Knopf, 1985.

Renninger, K. Ann, Suzanne Hidi, and Andreas Krapp, eds. *The Role of Interest in Learning and Development.* Hillsdale, N.J.: Lawrence Erlbaum, 1992.

Rheingold, Howard. *They Have a Word for It: A Lighthearted Lexicon of Untranslatable Words and Phrases.* Los Angeles: J. P. Tarcher, 1988.

Stein, Morris I. *Stimulating Creativity.* New York: Academic Press; Lawrence Erlbaum, 1974, 1975.

Tiedt, Iris M., Jo Ellen Carlson, Bert D. Howard, and Kathleen S. Oda Watanabe. *Teaching Thinking in K–12 Classrooms: Ideas, Activities, and Resources.* Boston: Allyn and Bacon, 1989.

Udall, Anne J., and Joan E. Daniels. *Creating the Thoughtful Classroom: Strategies to Promote Student Thinking.* Tucson, Ariz.: Zephyr Press, 1991.

Ury, William. *Getting Past No: Negotiating Your Way from Confrontation to Cooperation.* New York: Bantam Books, 1993.

Vaughan, Frances E. *Awakening Intuition.* New York: Doubleday, 1979.

von Oech, Roger. *A Kick in the Seat of the Pants.* New York: Harper and Row, 1986.

——. *A Whack on the Side of the Head,* 2nd ed. New York: Warner Books, 1990.

Watts, Alan. *The Book: On the Taboo against Knowing Who You Are.* New York: Collier Books, 1966.

Weinert, Franz E., and Rainer H. Kluwe, eds. *Metacognition, Motivation, and Understanding.* Hillsdale, N.J.: Lawrence Erlbaum, 1987.

White, Robert W. "Motivation Reconsidered: The Concept of Competence." *Psychological Review* 66 (1959): 297–333.

# Index

# Additional Resources from Zephyr Press

## CREATING THE THOUGHTFUL CLASSROOM

**Strategies to Promote Student Thinking**
by Anne J. Udall, Ph.D., and Joan E. Daniels, M.A.

This classroom-ready guide shows you how to develop your students' thinking skills. You'll have an overview of current models of thinking skills, practical techniques for your classroom, and ways to evaluate higher-level thinking.

To get started, you'll get answers to questions like—

- How much time will I need to teach thinking when I have so little time already?
- How do I successfully teach content and thinking processes at the same time?
- What does a "thoughtful classroom" look like?

Nine teacher strategies focus on a classroom environment that fosters complex thinking. You'll also become aware of nine student behaviors that reflect the development of higher-order thought.

*For teachers of grades 3–12.*
*168 pages, 8 1/2" x 11", softbound.*
**ZB22-W . . . $25**

## CREATING THE THOUGHTFUL CLASSROOM POSTERS

This handy set of 10 colorful posters will keep your class thinking about thinking. Posters 1 through 9 remind the student of the nine student behaviors described in the popular book *Creating the Thoughtful Classroom* by showing—

- An affirmation of each behavior for the student
- A quotation from a famous thinker that relates to the particular behavior

*10 full-color posters, printed on lightweight posterboard, each one 11" x 17"; clear storage bag.*
**ZM09-W . . $25**
SPECIAL OFFER—Order both the Thoughtful Classroom book and 10 posters and save $5.00.
**ZO09-W . . . $45.00**

## HOW TO BECOME AN EXPERT

**Discover, Research, and Build a Project in Your Chosen Field**
by Maurice Gibbons

Guide your students through the stages of becoming an expert in areas that they define. They start by becoming explorers then specialists . . . then apprentices who create products related to their areas of expertise.

Your students will learn to empower themselves to set their own goals, make plans for reaching those goals, and then follow through with their plans to the best of their abilities. They'll get lots of encouragement—and even a few laughs!

*Grades 5–8.*
*136 pages, 8 1/2" x 11", softbound.*
**ZB16-W . . . $19.95**

## RHYTHMS OF LEARNING

**Creative Tools for Developing Lifelong Skills**
by Don G. Campbell and Chris Boyd Brewer

Here are more than 75 classroom activities to boost learning and provide opportunities for personal growth.

Learn about the physical and emotional highs and lows to promote a learning environment that is less stressful and more focused. Specific activities for teachers precede and complement the student activities.

- Discover the best learning modes of your students
- Learn to use music, art, movement, and drama to promote optimal learning states
- Use effective rhythms of presentation in your teaching
- Learn about and use the methods of Lozanov and Tomatis and the techniques of accelerated learning

*Grades K–Adult.*
*320 pages, 7" x 9", softbound.*
**ZB21-W . . . $24.95**

## COACHING SCIENCE STARS

**Pep Talk and Play Book for Real-World Problem Solving**
by Robert C. Barkman, Ph.D.

Here's a sourcebook that brings to life the inquiry approach to science teaching.

- Promote cooperative learning
- Explore "real-life" problems
- Encourage critical and creative thinking
- Get students excited about science

Each of the four units models the philosophy of a problem-solving approach to science and offers 10 or more specific classroom activities that require only everyday items. You'll also have guidelines for creating your own science units that can encourage your students to think like scientists.
*Grades 6–12.*
*164 pages, 8 1/2" x 11", softbound.*
**ZB20-W . . . $17.95**

**To order, write or call—**

Zephyr Press
P.O. Box 66006-W
Tucson, Arizona 85728-6006
Phone—(602) 322-5090
FAX—(602) 323-9402

Please add 10% for shipping and handling costs to all orders.

You can also request a free copy of our current catalog showing other learning materials that foster whole-brain learning, creative thinking, and self-awareness.